The BEST JOKE BOOK

(period)

HUNDREDS OF THE FUNNIEST, SILLIEST, MOST RIDICULOUS JOKES EVER

William Donohue

Adams Media

New York   London   Toronto   Sydney   New Delhi

Adams Media
An Imprint of Simon & Schuster, Inc.
57 Littlefield Street
Avon, Massachusetts 02322

For information about special discounts for bulk purchases, please contact Simon & Schuster Special Sales at 1-866-506-1949 or business@simonandschuster.com.

The Simon & Schuster Speakers Bureau can bring authors to your live event. For more information or to book an event contact the Simon & Schuster Speakers Bureau at 1-866-248-3049 or visit our website at www.simonspeakers.com.

Interior images © iStockphoto.com and 123RF

Manufactured in the United States of America

10 2021

ISBN 978-1-4405-8309-4
ISBN 978-1-4405-8310-0 (ebook)

CONTENTS

INTRODUCTION

Stop me if you've heard this one before.

Knock-knock.

How many politicians does it to take to . . . ?

A guy walks into a bar.

While some jokes aren't for everyone, everyone loves a laugh.

And what better way to elicit some giggles than by sharing a good joke? Having some funny jokes up your sleeve can prove handy on any number of occasions. Jokes can help break the ice at parties, pass the time between business meetings, and even help impress a first date. Who doesn't love a quick wit and a sharp tongue? But if you're lacking in those qualities, don't fret. That's what these jokes are for!

Welcome to the wonderful world of jokes—a skill, an art, a way of life as old as time itself. Historians have traced jokes back as far as 1900 B.C. in ancient Sumer. And what did they laugh about in ancient times? You guessed it—the old standby of bathroom humor. Some things will always be a gas, it seems. But a good joke is hard to come by! Luckily for you, we're here to pull together a broad range of funny stuff so you have an arsenal of jokes at your disposal.

So whether you're looking to add a few jokes to your repertoire, improve your banter, or stockpile funny fodder for daily life, this is the book for you. Everyone knows a joke or two, but *The Best Joke Book (Period)* will give you a joke for every situation!

So pull up a chair and start learning some one-liners, quips, cracks, ribs, and yarns. Now's the time to get serious about joking—no funny business.

All in the Family:

Jokes about those we love to tease

They're with us through thick and thin—even when we wish they weren't! Brothers, sisters, mothers, fathers, cousins, and so on. These are the people who were there from the beginning and the people we will grow old with. Enjoy these jokes at the expense of your own flesh and blood!

I always carry a picture of my wife and kids in my wallet. I do it to remind myself why there is no money in there.

A man pulls over to the side of the road after a police cruiser flashes him to do so. "How long have you been riding around without a taillight?" asked the officer. "Oh, no!" screamed the man, jumping out of the car. "Wait 'til my family finds out!" "Where's your family?" the officer asked. "They're in the trailer that was hitched to the car!"

"I was the kid next door's imaginary friend."

—EMO PHILIPS

A man in the grocery store notices a woman with a three-year-old girl in her cart. As they pass the cookie section, the little girl screams for cookies. The mother says, "Now Missy, we only have a few more aisles to go—don't throw a fit. It won't be long." In the candy aisle, the little girl whines for candy. The mother says, "There, there, Missy, don't cry. Two more aisles, and we'll be checking out." When they get to the checkout stand, the little girl howls for gum. The mother says, reassuringly, "Missy, we'll be done in five minutes, and then you can go home and have a bottle and a nice snooze." In the parking lot, the man stops the woman to compliment her. "I couldn't help noticing how patient you were with little Missy," he says. The mother sighs, "Oh, no—my little girl's name is Francine. I'm Missy."

The odd thing about parenting is that by the time you are experienced at your job, you are unemployed.

A mother traveled across the country to watch her only son get married and graduate from the air force on the exact same day. "Thank you for coming," the son said. "It means so much." "Of course I'd be here," the mother replied. "It's not every day a mom watches her son get his wings and have them clipped all in one day."

A family takes a trip to Disney World. After seven exhausting days, they head home. As they drive away, the son waves out the window and says, "Goodbye, Mickey." The daughter waves and says, "Goodbye, Minnie." Dad waves and cries, "Goodbye, money."

Sarah watches as her mother tries on an expensive fur coat in a high-end department store. "Do you realize," Sarah says, "that some poor, dumb animal had to suffer just for you to wear that coat?" Sarah's mother turns to her and snaps, "Think about how much I've suffered! And don't call your father an animal."

Passing through his son's college town late one night, a father decides to drop in and pay his kid a visit. The father knocks on the fraternity house door. No one answers. He knocks louder, but still no answer. He begins to bang angrily on the door. Finally, a head pops out of a window on the second floor. "You need something, pal?" a frat brother asks from the window.

"Yes, does Billy Powers live here?" the father asks.

"Yeah," says the frat brother, "just dump him on the steps and we'll grab him in the morning."

"Then we figured out we could just park them in front of the TV; that's how I was raised and I turned out TV."—HOMER SIMPSON

A dad was trying to teach his kid about the evils of drinking. He put one worm in a glass of water and another worm in a glass of whiskey. The worm in the water survived, but the worm in the whiskey curled up and died almost immediately. "All right, kid," the father began, "what does this little experiment prove to you about drinking?"

"Well," the kid replied thoughtfully, "it proves that if a person drinks alcohol he probably won't get worms."

A guy calls 911 in a panic. "My wife is having a baby! Her contractions are only one minute apart!"

"Calm down," the 911 operator says. "Is this her first child?"

"No, you idiot!" the guy shouts. "This is her husband!"

How is a computer like a grandparent? *The first thing that goes on both is their memory.*

What does a baby computer call his father? *Data!*

A little girl asks her mother, "How did the human race appear?" The mother answers, "Well, God made Adam and Eve and then they had kids. So all mankind was made." Two days later the little girl asks her father the exact same question. The father answers, "Many years ago, there were monkeys from which the entire human race evolved." The confused little girl returns to her mother and says, "Mom, you told me the human race was created by God, and Dad said man developed from monkeys. Why do you have different stories?" The mother answers, "Well, I was referring to my side of the family and your dad was talking about his side."

> **"When my parents got divorced, there was a custody fight over me . . . no one showed up."**—RODNEY DANGERFIELD

The three wise men visit Joseph and Mary in the stable to see the newborn son. The extremely tall wise man hits his head on the door frame and exclaims, "Jesus Christ!" Joseph looks at Mary and says, "Write that down—that's much better than Clyde."

———◆———

A small boy swallows some coins and is taken to a hospital. When his grandmother telephones to ask how he is, the nurse tells her, "No change yet."

———◆———

Two boys are arguing when the teacher enters the classroom. The teacher says, "What are you two arguing about?"

One boy answers, "We found a ten-dollar bill and decided whoever tells the biggest lie gets to keep it."

"You two should be ashamed of yourselves," said the teacher. "When I was your age, I didn't even know what a lie was." The boys looked at each other and handed the ten dollars to the teacher.

"A two-year-old is kind of like having a blender, but you don't have a top for it."—JERRY SEINFELD

A young boy runs into the house and excitedly shows his mother a fifty-dollar bill he found in the park. "Are you sure it was lost?" the mother asks.

"I'm positive," the boy replies. "I even saw the guy looking for it."

———◆———

A teacher asks her class, "True or false? The Declaration of Independence was written in Philadelphia."

"False," says a boy in the back. "It was written in ink."

———◆———

A teacher walks over to the desk of a student during an exam and says to him, "I hope I didn't just see you looking over at your neighbor's answers."

The boy replies, "Yeah, I hope you didn't see it either."

———◆——

A school teacher notices a student is getting much better with numbers than he was just a few weeks earlier. "Your counting has improved," the teacher tells him after class.

"Thanks," the boy says. "My dad will be glad to hear that. He's been working on them with me every night and weekend."

"Fantastic," the teacher replies. "So here's a quick quiz—what comes after nine?"

"Ten," the boy replies enthusiastically.

"Right, and what comes after ten?" the teacher quizzes.

"The jack!" the boy answers.

"We have a beautiful little girl who we named after my mom; in fact, Passive Aggressive Psycho turns five tomorrow."—STEWART FRANCIS

A husband and wife are visiting the wife's family during the holidays. Her mother is a stickler for her food intake, and will only eat organic and fresh foods. The husband goes to the store with specific instructions on the type of foods to buy. "Excuse me," the man asks the grocer, "are these vegetables sprayed with any harmful chemicals or pesticides that could kill a person?" "Nope," answers the grocer proudly. "Okay," says the man, "I guess I'll just have to do that part myself."

———◆———

A second-grade teacher is giving her daily grammar lesson. "Tammy," the teacher calls out to a girl in the first row of class, "please use 'I' in a sentence."

"I is," Tammy begins, but was immediately interrupted.

"No, Tammy," the teacher says, "that's incorrect. You always say 'I am.'"

"All right," Tammy says. "I am the letter that comes after H."

———◆———

A church pastor is invited to dinner at the house of a parishioner. The pastor sits at the table with the family. The mom requests her daughter, age six, say grace before the meal. She sits in silence. "It's okay, dear," the mother calms her. "You can do it. Just repeat what you heard daddy say before breakfast this morning."

The little girl folds her hands, bows her head, and says in a loud voice, "Oh Christ, why did you invite the pastor over for dinner tonight?"

———◆———

During a dinner party, the hosts' two little children enter the dining room totally nude and walk slowly around the table. The parents are so embarrassed that they pretend nothing is happening and keep the conversation going. The guests cooperate and also continue as if nothing extraordinary is happening. After going all the way around the room the children leave, and there is a moment of silence at the table, during which one of the children is heard saying, "You see, it is vanishing cream!"

"Mothers are fonder than fathers of their children because they are more certain they are their own."—ARISTOTLE

A kid is late for school one day. "I had to take the bull down to mate with the heifer," he explains to the teacher.

"Well, couldn't your father have done that?" the teacher asks after class.

"Sure," the boy replies. "But the bull would have done a better job."

A father confronts his young son in the backyard. "I heard you skipped school today to go to the beach with your friends."

"That's a lie!" the boy shouts. "And I've got the movie stub to prove it."

———◆———

Children left alone in the backseat can cause accidents, which is ironic considering that accidents in the backseat can cause children.

———◆———

A stranger at the park is watching a young boy play in front of his young mother. After a few minutes of the boy clucking incessantly, the man asks, "Why does your son repeatedly say 'cluck, cluck, cluck'?"

The young mother replies, "Because he thinks he's a chicken."

"Why don't you tell him he's not a chicken?" the stranger asks.

"Well," says the mom, "because we really need the eggs."

"My dad is actually a manic-depressive, which is very exciting half the time."—MARC MARON

Four expectant fathers pace back and forth in a hospital waiting room while their wives are in labor. The nurse enters and tells the first man, "Congratulations, you're the father of twins!"

"What a coincidence," the man says. "I work for the Minnesota Twins baseball team."

A little later, the nurse returns and tells the second man, "You are the father of triplets!"

"That's really an incredible coincidence," he answers, "considering I work for the 3M Company."

An hour later, the nurse tells the third man that his wife has just given birth to quadruplets. The man says, "That's insane! I work for the Four Seasons. What a weird coincidence!"

After hearing this latest news, everyone's attention turns to the fourth expectant father, who has just fainted. He slowly regains consciousness and whispers to the attending nurse, "I knew I shouldn't have taken that job at Books-A-Million."

> **"Having children is like living in a frat house: nobody sleeps, everything's broken, and there's a lot of throwing up."**
>
> —RAY ROMANO

A young boy is listening to the radio in the car with his father. "Dad, what music did you like growing up?"

"I was a huge fan of Led Zeppelin," the father replies.

"Who?" the son asks.

"Yeah," the dad responds, "I liked them too."

A teacher asks her class their favorite afterschool snacks. "Decklyn," the teacher calls to the new student in the back of the room, "what's your favorite afterschool snack?"

"Nuts," he replies.

"Very good," the teacher replies. "What kind of nuts? Peanuts? Pine nuts?"

The boy shakes his head and answers, "Doughnuts."

Two young boys, Bobby and Tommy, are sharing a hospital room. After getting to know each other a little bit, Bobby eventually asks Tommy, "Hey, what're you in the hospital for anyway?"

"I'm getting my tonsils out," explains Tommy. "And I'm a little worried."

"Oh, don't worry about it," Bobby says. "I had my tonsils out and it was actually not so bad. I got to eat all the ice cream and Jell-O I wanted for two weeks!"

"Oh yeah?" replies Tommy. "That's not bad. So, Bobby, how about you? What are you here for?"

"I'm getting a circumcision, whatever that is," Bobby answers.

"Oh my god! A circumcision?" Tommy cries. "I got one of those when I was a baby. I couldn't walk for two years!"

"Fatherhood is great because you can ruin someone from scratch."—JON STEWART

A lifeguard asks a mother to scold her son for urinating in the public pool. "It's perfectly natural," the mother says, "for young children to urinate in the pool. Plenty of children at this pool do it. I don't see why my son doing it is such a big deal."

The lifeguard pulls down his sunglasses and replies, "Well, all the other kids aren't doing it off the diving board."

"When I was kidnapped my parents snapped into action . . . they rented out my room."—WOODY ALLEN

A teenager is talking to her friend before class. "For the prom, I'm renting a limo, spending $500 on a new dress, and bringing in the best makeup artist in the state to do my hair."

A teacher overhears the conversation and remarks, "Wow, that's more than I spent for my wedding!"

The girl replies, "Yeah, well you can get married three or four times, but you only go to prom once."

———◆———

On his eighteenth birthday, a son announces to his parents that he is no longer abiding by their curfew. "I'm an adult now," he says, "and you can't stop me from exiting and entering the house any time I want."

"You're half right," says his dad. "We can't stop you from leaving the house, but we can stop you from coming back in."

"How dare you disobey your mother!" a father yells at his daughter. "Do you think you're better than I am or something?"

"How did the car end up in the living room?" a furious father asks his son.

"Simple," the boy replies. "I made a right at the kitchen."

A teen is caught smoking pot behind a local convenience store. He's arrested and put in county jail. The arresting officer advises the young pothead that he gets one phone call from jail. The teen makes his phone call and returns to his cell. About a half hour later a man shows up at the police station. "I assume you're the boy's father," the arresting officer says.

"No," responds the man, "I'm here to deliver a pizza."

Two young girls, students at an exclusive prep school in California, are eating lunch and flipping through a celebrity magazine.

"Oh my god, I forgot to tell you!" the blonde says to the brunette. "My mom is getting remarried!"

"No way," the brunette replies. "To who?"

The blonde flips open the magazine and points to a famous director.

"Oh!" screams the brunette. "You'll love him! He was my dad last year!"

"Any kid will run any errand for you, if you ask at bedtime."—RED SKELTON

A freshman is talking to the new girl in school. "You'll like it here," he tells her. "Everyone is pretty chill, the teachers are all nice, but the principal is kind of a moron."

"Do you know who I am?" the girl asks her new classmate. "I'm the daughter of the principal."

The boy is silent and then asks her, "Do you know who I am?"

She shakes her head no. "Good," says the boy as he walks away.

A teacher asks her student where the English Channel is located. "I'm not sure," the student answers, "we switched cable companies last month."

A father goes into his son's room to find him lying face-down on the bed. He asks him, "Hey buddy, how did your test go today?"

"I did just what George Washington did," the son replies, his words muffled by the mattress.

"How so?" the father asks.

The son looks up and answers, "I went down in history."

A father and mother send their son to a special tutor because he's falling behind in school. After weeks of personal classes and hundreds of dollars, the parents ask the tutor for a progress report. "Good news," the tutor tells them over the phone, "your son is getting straight As."

"That's outstanding!" says the father.

"I'll say," the tutor replies. "I think we're finally ready to move on to the letter B."

What's the difference between a teenager and E.T.?
E.T. actually phoned home.

How many teenagers does it take to screw in a light bulb?
One. He holds the bulb up and the world revolves around him.

"Many children threaten at times to run away from home—this is the only thing that keeps many parents going."—PHYLLIS DILLER

Grandma and Grandpa are trying to console Susie, whose dog, Skipper, has died. "You know," Grandma said, "it's not so bad. Skipper's probably up in heaven right now, having a grand old time with God." Susie stops crying and asks, "What would God want with a dead dog?"

"You're not famous until my mother has heard of you."—JAY LENO

On a visit to see his grandmother, a teen boy listens as she goes on and on about the cost of living. "When I was a young girl," she moans, "you could go to the store with a dollar and come home with enough food to feed your family for weeks!"

"Well, Grandma," the boy replies, "we learned about that in school recently, and that's called inflation."

"Inflation nothing!" the grandmother answered. "It's all these darn security cameras they've got today!"

———•—•———

Ted's grandmother pulls him aside at his eighth birthday party and hands the boy a five-dollar bill. "Here, this is a little something extra from Grandma. But not a word of this to your brothers and sisters."

The boy looks at the bill and responds, "If you want me to stay quiet, it's going to cost you a lot more."

———•—•———

How many Jewish grandmothers does it take to screw in a light bulb? *None, because never mind us, we'll just sit here in the dark, don't go out of your way . . . "*

A husband and wife are staring at their garden. "Sooner or later," the wife comments, "you're going to have to put in a better scarecrow."

"What's wrong with the one we've got?" asks the husband. "It scares away all the birds and it's still got a few good years left."

"I agree," the wife says, "but my mother can't stay out there forever."

"The tooth fairy teaches children that they can sell body parts for money."—DAVID RICHERBY

"Hi! My name is Gertrude," says the lady to the man next to her on the airplane. "It's so nice to meet you! I'm flying to New York for my grandson's third birthday. I'm so excited! I remember when he was just a little pumpkin and now he's already three! It's really hard to believe. He's the most adorable thing you've ever seen! You know what? Hold on, I think I might have a picture on me. Let me take a look in my purse. Yes, here it is. Just look at him, isn't he adorable? Do you see his dimple on his left cheek? Simply adorable! I could stare at his picture all day. Oh my, and you should hear him on the phone! He is just the cutest. He says to me in the cutest voice, 'Hi Grandma!' It just gets me all teary-eyed." After what seemed like two hours for the poor man sitting next to her, Gertrude realized that perhaps she was talking a bit too much.

"You know, I feel terrible! Here I am just talking and talking without letting you get in a word edgewise! Tell me, what do you think about my grandson?"

"When I was a boy, I laid in my twin sized bed, wondering where my brother was."—MITCH HEDBERG

A young boy finds his grandfather, an avid gardener, working in his garden one afternoon. "What do you usually put on your celery?" the boy asks his grandfather. The old man wipes the sweat and dirt from his forehead. He's amazed his grandson has taken such an interest in his hobby. "Well, I usually put on a mix of enriched soil and rotted horse manure." "That's weird," the grandson replies. "We usually just put on ranch dressing."

———◆———

A family moves into their new house. Grandma comes for a visit and asks the youngest child, a five-year-old, how he likes the new place. "It's terrific," he says. "I have my own room, my brother has his own room, and my sister has her own room. But poor mom is still sleeping with dad."

A man comes home one night to find his blonde wife reading his personal journal.

"I can explain everything," he begins. She interrupts him midsentence and exclaims, "You're darn right you've got some explaining to do, and you can start with telling me who April, May, and June are!"

"The only truly anonymous donor is the guy who knocks up your daughter."
—LENNY BRUCE

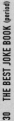

Chapter 2

LOVE AND MARRIAGE:

Jokes for married folks

F rank Sinatra once sang that love and marriage was an institute you can't disparage. Well, Ol' Blue Eyes was half right. It might be difficult to make jokes about love, but you can make jokes about marriage, because there's plenty to laugh at. Not to mention the pitfalls of dating, cheating, rejection, and breakups! Now *there* is some material.

Why do peppers make bad girlfriends? *Because they are constantly jalapeño business.*

After traveling on business, Tim thinks it would be nice to bring his girlfriend a little gift. "How about some perfume?" he asks the cosmetics clerk. She shows him a fifty-dollar bottle.

"That's a bit much," says Tim, so she returns with a smaller bottle for thirty dollars.

"That's still quite a bit," Tim complains. Growing annoyed, the clerk brings out a tiny fifteen-dollar bottle.

"What I mean," said Tim, "is I'd like to see something really cheap." So the clerk handed him a mirror.

"Marriage is the death of hope."
—WOODY ALLEN

A police officer finds a young couple messing around in their parked car. The officer shines his light into the window. The young man jumps out of the car and claims, "Honest, officer, we weren't doing anything."

"In that case," the officer replies, "let me inside and you come here and hold the flashlight."

"Lately, I think that my wife has been fooling around because our parrot keeps saying, 'Give it to me hard and fast before my husband, Jon Katz, comes home; and, yes, I'd love a cracker.'"—JONATHAN KATZ

While visiting a friend in the hospital, a young man notices several gorgeous nurses, each one of them wearing a pin designed to look like an apple. "What does the pin signify?" he asks one of them.

"Oh, nothing," she says with a chuckle. "We just use it to keep the doctors away."

A man cheats on his girlfriend, Lorraine, with a girl named Clearly. Suddenly, Lorraine dies. At the funeral, the man stands up and sings loudly, "I can see Clearly now, Lorraine is gone."

Never date a radiologist. She'll see right through you.

What was Adam and Eve's biggest problem during their marriage? *They could never agree on who wore the plants in the family.*

A woman is having lunch in a Los Angeles cafe when a man approaches her table. "Excuse me, miss," the man says, "my wife and I are visiting from out of town. She loves your sandals. She wanted me to come over and ask if you bought those sandals around here."

"Actually," the woman responds, "I got them in a shop just about a block from here."

"Fantastic," the man responds, "and if I may ask, how much did you pay for them?"

"I paid $250," she admits.

"Thank you," the man responds. He walks away and yells to his wife, "She got them in New York!"

A husband and wife are in line at the grocery store. The clerk asks if they have a preferred shopper's card.

"Yes," says the wife, "but I left it at home."

The clerk says they could look it up by birthday. The woman gives her birthday, but they can't find her card in the system. After a few more tries, they ask her more information, until her account finally comes up on the computer.

"I think I see the issue," the clerk said. "Someone put your birthday in the system as 6/24/1899."

"Obviously, that's wrong," the woman says.

The husband finally breaks his silence and adds, "She was born in September of that year, not June."

"Paying alimony is like feeding hay to a dead horse." —GROUCHO MARX

A young couple are trying to save money on their summer vacation. They bring their bags to the discount airline desk to check in.

"Do you have reservations?" asks the woman behind the counter.

"More than a few," the young man answered, "but we're flying with you guys anyway."

"My toughest fight was with my first wife."
—MUHAMMAD ALI

A couple is sitting on the porch sipping wine. The wife says, "I love you."

The husband says, "Is that you or the wine talking?"

The wife replies, "It's me, talking to the wine."

A wife goes to the police station with her next-door neighbor to report that her husband is missing. The policeman asks for a description. She says, "He's thirty-five years old, six foot four, has dark eyes, dark wavy hair, an athletic build, weighs 185 pounds, is soft-spoken, and is good to the children."

The next-door neighbor protests, "Your husband is five foot four, chubby, bald, has a big mouth, and is mean to your children."

The wife replies, "Yes, but who wants *him* back?"

Early in the morning, a wife turns over to find her husband wide awake in bed.

"Are you okay?" the wife asks.

"I guess," he replies.

"I'm asking because you spent the entire night cursing me in your sleep."

The man replies, "Who said I was asleep?"

"If you can't live without me, why aren't you dead already?"—CYNTHIA HEIMEL

A drunk husband wakes up from another all-night bender and stumbles into the kitchen.

"I'm guessing you feel awful again this morning," his wife snaps.

"Actually, I feel good," the husband responds. "I slept like a log."

"You didn't even come to bed," the wife answers.

"I know," he answers. "I passed out in the fireplace."

Two men are drinking at a bar all night. Finally, one man says to the other, "I hate to break up the fun, but I've got to go home and take off my wife's underwear."

The other man replies, "What makes you think you'll be so lucky?"

The first man replies while walking out the door, "because they've been riding up my butt all night and I've had enough."

———◆———

A husband and wife are sitting at a table at her twentieth high-school reunion. There is an incredibly drunk man slumped over at the table across from them.

"Do you know that guy?" the husband asks.

"Yes," the wife replies somberly. "That's my ex-boyfriend. He started drinking right after we broke up and hasn't been sober since."

"Good God," the husband replies. "Who knew it was possible to celebrate for that long?"

> **"If you talk about yourself, he'll think you're boring; if you talk about others, he'll think you're a gossip; if you talk about *him*, he'll think you're a brilliant conversationalist."**—LINDA SUNSHINE

A man is explaining to his coworker that he never realized how much his wife loved him until he was home sick from work the previous day.

"Really?" the coworker asks. "What showed you she really loved you?"

"She was just really excited to have me around," the man replied. "Like when the mailman and FedEx guy came to the door she shouted excitedly, 'My husband is home! My husband is home!'"

Two men are sitting in a sauna after a workout. "I'll be honest, my wife really is an angel."

"You're lucky," the second man answers, wiping the sweat from his brow. "My wife is still alive."

"When I invite a woman to dinner, I expect her to look at my face; that's the price she has to pay."—GROUCHO MARX

"I can't believe you're sleeping with my best friend!" a husband yells at his wife while packing up his belongings.

"Does the fact that he finds me attractive really surprise you?" the wife asks.

"Yes," the man replies, "especially after everything I've told him!"

"It's really hot outside," a husband tells his wife, staring out the front window. "What do you think the neighbors would think if I mowed the lawn naked?" he asks jokingly.

The wife replies without looking up from the morning paper, "They'll probably think I married you for the money."

"Husbands are chiefly good lovers when they are betraying their wives."—MARILYN MONROE

A husband is late coming home one night and isn't answering his cell phone. His wife calls her mother, incredibly upset. "I'm afraid he's having an affair," she tells her mother.

"Why do you always think the worst?" her mother asks. "Maybe he just got in a car crash or something."

The guest of honor at an awards dinner is about to give his speech when a stagehand gives him a piece of paper from his wife in the crowd.

"What does it say?" the stagehand asks.

"Oh, it just says KISS in very big letters."

"Wow, that's very sweet," the stagehand replies. "She must love you and be very proud of you."

"Not really," the man says. "It stands for Keep It Short, Stupid."

A man is staggering home drunk after last call. A policeman sees the man stumbling around and asks where he's going.

"I'm heading to a lecture," the man slurs in response.

"A lecture?" the skeptical cop responds. "Who would be giving a lecture at this time of the night?"

"My wife," the drunk man answers.

Matt's wife has been dropping hints about her birthday gift for weeks. Now, on the day before, Matt asks, "So what do you think you're getting for your birthday?"

His wife responds, "All I know is that it better be in the driveway and it better go from zero to 200 in under six seconds."

"Oh, it will," Matt responds, "and it does."

The next morning his wife wakes up to find a bathroom scale in the driveway.

"My mother always said don't marry for money, divorce for money."—WENDY LIEBMAN

An Amish boy and his father are visiting a nearby mall. They are amazed by almost everything they see, but especially by two shiny silver walls that move apart and back together again by themselves.

The lad asks, "What is this, father?"

The father, having never seen an elevator, responds, "I have no idea what it is."

While the boy and his father are watching wide-eyed, an old lady in a wheel-chair rolls up to the moving walls and presses a button. The walls open and the lady rolls between them into a small room. The walls close and the boy and his father watch as small circles light up above the walls. The walls open up again and a beautiful twenty-four-year-old woman steps out. The father looks at his son excitedly and says, "Go get your mother."

A woman calls her husband at work to share some news. "I'm kind of busy right now, babe, can't it wait until I get home?"

"Not really," she replies. "I've just got to share some good news and some bad news."

"All right," he replies, playing along. "I'm in a rush, so just give me the good news."

"Well," she sighs, "the good news is that the airbags on the car work correctly."

———

A husband and wife celebrate being married for fifty years and never getting into an argument. The husband asks his wife, "How did you make it through all those years without getting into an argument?"

The old woman says every time she got mad at her husband, she would sew a doily, and it would calm her down. The next day, the husband and wife are cleaning out a closet and the husband finds a box with one doily and a stack of money totaling $25,000. He is excited to find the money, but also happy that after all these years, his wife has only gotten mad at him one time.

He asks his wife about the contents of the box. She says, "Well, the doily is from just last week, when you forgot to pick me up from the doctor's office, and the money is from the past fifty years of selling doilies."

"I never mind my wife having the last word; in fact, I'm delighted when she gets to it."
—WALTER MATTHAU

A man hates his wife's cat with a passion and decides to get rid of it once and for all. He drives twenty blocks away from home and drops the cat there. The cat is already walking up the driveway as the man approaches his house. The next day, he decides to drop the cat forty blocks away, but the same thing happens. He keeps on increasing the number of blocks, but the cat keeps on coming home before him.

At last he decides to drive a few miles away, turn right, then left, past the bridge, then right again, and another right and so on until he reaches what he thinks is a perfect spot and drops the cat there. Hours later, the man calls his wife at home and asks her, "Jen, is the cat there?"

"Yes, why do you ask?" answers the wife.

Frustrated, the man says, "Put that cat on the phone. I'm lost and I need directions."

———•—•———

A married couple looks over the side of a wishing well. The guy leans over, makes a wish, and throws in a penny. His wife decides to make a wish, too, but she leans over too far, falls into the well, and drowns. The guy says, "Wow, it really works."

———•—•———

A man goes into a restaurant. He has a seat at a booth and opens a menu to find out that none of the foods have prices next to them. He asks the waiter, "How much is the Fettuccine Alfredo?"

The waiter says, "A penny."

The man exclaims, "A penny? How much for a steak?"

The waiter says, "A nickel." The man is astonished.

"Are you serious? Where's the man who owns this place? I'd like to shake his hand!"

The waiter answers, "He's upstairs with my wife."

Confused, the man asks, "What's he doing upstairs with your wife?"

The waiter smiles and says, "The same thing I'm doing down here to his business."

"I've often wanted to drown my troubles, but I can't get my wife to go swimming."
—JIMMY CARTER

A man is sitting at home when a police officer knocks on his door. The officer asks him if he is married and the man replies, "Yes, I am." The officer then asks him if he has a recent picture of his wife. The man answers, "Sure, hold on a second." The officer looks at the picture, and in a sad voice says, "I'm sorry, but it looks like your wife has been hit by a train."

The man says, "I know, but she has a good personality."

After thirty years of marriage a husband and wife go for counseling. When asked what the problem is, the wife goes into a tirade listing every problem they had ever had in the years they had been married. On and on she goes: neglect, lack of intimacy, emptiness, loneliness, feeling unloved and unlovable—an entire laundry list of unmet needs she has endured. Finally, after allowing this for a sufficient length of time, the therapist gets up, walks around the desk, and after asking the wife to stand, he embraces and kisses her long and passionately as her husband watches with a raised eyebrow. The woman shuts up and quietly sits down as though in a daze. The therapist turns to the husband and says, "This is what your wife needs at least three times a week. Can you do this?"

"Well, I can drop her off here on Mondays and Wednesdays, but on Fridays, I fish."

A very elderly couple is celebrating their seventy-fifth wedding anniversary. The man says to his wife, "Dear, there is something that I must ask you. It has always bothered me that our tenth child never looked quite like the rest. Now, I want to assure you that these seventy-five years have been the most wonderful experience I could have ever hoped for, and your answer could not take all of that away. But, I must know, did he have a different father?"

The wife drops her head, unable to look her husband in the eye, and then confesses. "Yes, he did."

The old man is very shaken, the reality hitting him harder than he expected. With a tear in his eye he asks, "Who? Who was he? Who was the father?"

Again the woman drops her head, saying nothing at first as she tries to muster the courage to tell the truth to her husband. Then, finally she says to her husband, "You."

An old man goes to his doctor and says, "I don't think my wife's hearing is as good as it used to be. What should I do?"

The doctor replies, "Try this test to find out for sure. When your wife is in the kitchen doing dishes, stand fifteen feet behind her and ask her a question. If she doesn't respond, keep moving closer, asking the question until she hears you."

The man goes home and sees his wife preparing dinner. He stands 15 feet behind her and says, "What's for dinner, honey?" No response. He moves to 10 feet behind her and asks again—no response. Five feet, no answer. Finally, he stands directly behind her and asks, "Honey, what's for supper?"

She says, "For the fourth time, I said chicken!"

"Husbands are awkward things to deal with; even keeping them in hot water will not make them tender."—MARY BUCKLEY

A husband and wife go to a restaurant. The waiter approaches the table to take their order. "I'll have your biggest, juiciest steak," says the husband.

"But sir, what about the mad cow?" asks the waiter.

"Oh," says the husband, "she'll order for herself."

———◆———

A man is on a cross-country trip when he picks up a hitchhiker. During a lull in the conversation, the hitchhiker notices a brown paper bag resting in the center console. The driver notices his glance and says, "That's a bottle of wine. I got it for my wife."

The hitchhiker replies, "That's a pretty good trade."

"When I meet a man I ask myself, 'Is this the man I want my children to spend their weekends with?'"—RITA RUDNER

A man phones home from the office and tells his wife, "Something has just come up. I need to go fishing with the boss for the weekend. We leave right away, so can you pack my clothes, my fishing equipment, and my blue silk pajamas? I'll be home in an hour to pick them up."

He hurries home, grabs everything, and rushes off. Sunday night, he returns. His wife asks, "Did you have a good trip?"

"Oh yes, great! I think I really impressed the boss. But you forgot to pack my blue silk pajamas."

"Oh, no I didn't. I put them in your tackle box."

What do you call a man who has lost 90 percent of his intelligence? *Divorced.*

Real men wear pink because that's what their wives bought.

A man goes away on business. He e-mails his wife from the road and says he'll be home that night because the trip wrapped up earlier than expected. When he gets home, he walks into the bedroom to find his wife in bed with another man. Without a word, the husband leaves the room and goes down to the local bar. He explains the whole situation to the bartender.

"Well, why don't you call her and talk to her? Maybe there is an explanation for all of this."

The man picks up his cell phone and calls his house. His wife answers and before she can say a word he yells, "Why did I come home to find you in bed with another man?" The wife calmly responds, "Because I just got around to checking my e-mail."

"Whenever you want to marry someone, go have lunch with his ex-wife."—SHELLEY WINTERS

A wife comes downstairs before a dinner date with her husband.

"Do I look fat in this dress?" the wife asked.

"Do I look dumb in this shirt?" the husband replied.

A woman walks into a pet store and sees a handsome bright red parrot. She asks the cashier how much the parrot is. The cashier says, "I'll sell it, but I should warn you, it was donated by a brothel, so it might have picked up some colorful language."

The woman says, "Oh, that's okay." She buys the parrot and takes it home.

When she takes the towel off its cage, the parrot looks at her and says, "Awk. New madam. Hello madam."

A few hours later, the woman's two teenage daughters come home from school. The parrot looks at them and says, "Awk. New girls. Hello girls."

A couple hours after that, the woman's husband Phil comes home from work. The parrot looks at him and says, "Awk. Hi Phil."

Chapter 3

HO-HO-HO-LIDAY:

Jokes for special occasions

Holidays are a time to be happy and enjoy the company of loved ones. What better way to spread cheer and goodwill than with a small arsenal of jokes perfect for the Christmas cocktail party or over a pint on St. Paddy's Day? These jokes about the holidays are sure to make everyone's belly shake like a bowl full of jelly!

The worst thing about office holiday parties is having to spend the entire day after looking for a new job.

Did you hear about the Advent calendar that passed away? *Its days were numbered.*

What do you call an elf that lives in Beverly Hills? *Welfy.*

"The one thing women don't want to find in their stockings on Christmas morning is their husband."—JOAN RIVERS

It was Christmas time, and the judge was feeling a little benevolent and filled with holiday spirit. "What exactly is the charge?" he asked counsel.

"The man standing before you is charged with doing his Christmas shopping early."

"Shopping early?" the judge replied. "Well, what's wrong with that?"

The prosecutor replied, "He was doing his shopping before the stores were open."

A man hands his girlfriend a small package on Christmas morning, the size of a jewelry box. The woman gets incredibly excited and rips the package open to find a deck of playing cards.

"What the heck is this?" she yells and throws the deck of cards into the man's lap. "What?" the man responds. "You said all you wanted for Christmas was something with diamonds in it!"

"I once wanted to become an atheist, but I gave up—they have no holidays."—HENNY YOUNGMAN

During the rush of the holiday season, Sarah completely forgot to mail a Christmas card to her best friend. She hurries into the post office with a card and asks the postal service worker for a first-class stamp.

"Do I have to put this stamp on myself?" she asks.

"No," the postal employee replies. "You can put it right on the envelope."

A guy bought his wife a beautiful diamond ring for Hanukkah. After hearing about this extravagant gift, a friend of his says, "I thought she wanted one of those sporty four-wheel-drive vehicles."

"She did," he replies. "But where was I going to find a fake Jeep?"

There are four stages of life that involve Santa Claus— first you believe in Santa Claus, then you stop believing in Santa Claus, then you become Santa Claus to your family, and then you look like Santa Claus.

A couple are Christmas shopping. The shopping center is packed, and as the wife walks through one of the stores, she is surprised when she looks around to find that her husband is nowhere to be seen. She is quite upset because they had a lot to do. She becomes so worried that she calls him to ask where he is. In a quiet voice he says, "Do you remember the jeweler's we went into about five years ago where you fell in love with that diamond necklace that we couldn't afford, and I told you that I would get it for you one day?"

The wife gets choked up and starts to cry and says, "Yes, I do remember that shop."

He replies, "Well, I'm in the pub next door."

"Santa Claus has the right idea—visit people only once a year."—VICTOR BORGE

What is the most popular Christmas wine? *"This isn't what I asked for!"*

———•———

Why was Santa's little helper depressed? *Because the poor fella had low elf esteem.*

———•———

What do you call a kid who doesn't believe in Santa? *A rebel without a Claus.*

"A lovely thing about Christmas is that it's compulsory, like a thunderstorm, and we all go through it together."

—GARRISON KEILLOR

Why is Christmas just like a day at work? *You do all the work and the fat guy with the suit gets all the credit.*

———————

What do you get when you cross a snowman with a vampire? *Frostbite.*

———————

On Christmas morning a woman tells her husband, "I just dreamed that you gave me a beautiful diamond necklace. What do you think it means?"

"You'll know tonight," he says. That evening just before opening presents, the husband comes home with a small package and gives it to his wife. Delighted, she opens it only to find a book titled *The Meaning of Dreams*.

"I stopped believing in Santa Claus when I was six. Mother took me to see him in a department store and he asked for my autograph."
—SHIRLEY TEMPLE

Admiring the Christmas trees displayed in his neighbors' windows, a child asks his father, "Daddy, can we have a Hanukkah tree?"

"What? No, of course not," says his father.

"Why not?" asks the child again.

Bewildered, his father replies, "Because the last time we had dealings with a lighted bush we spent forty years wandering the desert."

The mall Santa had many children asking for electric trains. "If you get a train," he tells each one, "you know your dad is going to want to play with it too. Is that okay?" After he asks that question of little Tommy, the boy becomes very quiet. Trying to move the conversation along, Santa asks what else he would like Santa to bring him. The boy promptly replies, "Another train."

> **"Once again, we come to the Holiday Season, a deeply religious time that each of us observes, in his own way, by going to the mall of his choice."**—DAVE BARRY

On the first day of Hanukkah, a grandmother is giving her grandson directions to her apartment. He is coming to visit with his new wife.

"You come to the front door of the condominium complex. I am in apartment 2B. There is a big panel at the front door. With your elbow, push button 2B. I'll buzz you in. Come inside and the elevator is on the right. Hit the up button with your elbow, get in, and with your other elbow hit the number two. When you exit the elevator, I'm the second door on the right. Ring my doorbell with your elbow and I'll let you in."

"Grandma, that sounds easy," replies the grandson. "But why am I hitting all these buttons with my elbow?"

His grandmother answers, "You're coming to visit empty-handed?"

———◆———

A woman goes to the post office for stamps for Hanukkah cards. She asks the cashier for stamps and the cashier replies, "What denomination?" The woman thinks for a moment and responds, "I'll take six Orthodox, twelve Conservative, and thirty-two Reform, please."

———◆———

A son is visiting his mother the week after Hanukkah wearing one of the two sweaters she'd given him as a gift for the holiday. As he walks into her house, instead of saying hello, the mother says, "What's wrong? You didn't like the other sweater I got you?"

"That's the true spirit of Christmas; people being helped by people other than me."—JERRY SEINFELD

A man wants Valentine's Day to be special, so he buys a bottle of absinthe and stops by the florist's to order a bouquet of his wife's favorite flower: white anemones. Unfortunately, the florist is sold out of flowers and has only a few stems of feathery ferns. The man asks the florist to make a bouquet out of the ferns and the flask of liquor. He adds a card and proceeds home. After a romantic candlelight dinner, he presents his wife with the gift. She opens the card to read, "Absinthe makes the heart grow fonder."

With a tear in her eye, she whispers to him lovingly, "Yes, and with fronds like these, who needs anemones?"

"Valentine's Day: the holiday that reminds you that if you don't have a special someone, you're alone."—LEWIS BLACK

A young man is waiting in line at a post office when he notices an older man in the corner of the office, licking stamps that say *Love* on them and putting them on bright pink envelopes. The man then takes a bottle of perfume from his jacket pocket and sprays the envelopes. Curiosity gets the better of the young man, so he walks over and asks the older man what he is doing. "I'm sending out five hundred Valentine's cards with the phrase 'Guess Who?' written inside."

"Why?" the young man asks.

The man smiles and says, "Because I'm a divorce lawyer."

Two antennae met on a roof on Valentine's Day. They fell in love and got married. Their wedding ceremony wasn't anything fancy, but the reception was awesome.

What do farmers give their wives on Valentine's Day? *Hogs and kisses.*

What is the difference between a calendar and you? *A calendar has a date on Valentine's day.*

What did the French chef give his wife for Valentine's Day? *A hug and a quiche.*

Did you know Valentine's Day is a huge holiday for skunks? *They are all very scent-imental.*

"It goes Christmas, New Year's Eve, Valentine's Day. Is that fair to anyone who's alone? These are all days you gotta be with someone. And if you didn't get around to killing yourself at Christmas or New Year's, boom! There's Valentine's Day. I think there should be one more after Valentine's Day just called, 'Who could love you?'"

—LAURA KIGHTLINGER

Why do leprechauns make great secretaries? *They've got great short hand.*

———•———

What type of lawn furniture is only used on St. Patrick's Day? *Paddy O'Furniture.*

———•———

Why is it always a bad idea to iron a four-leaf clover? *Because you should never press your luck.*

A priest is driving home from the bar on St. Patrick's Day. He mistakenly takes an empty bottle of wine with him and tosses it onto the floor on the passenger side of the car. He's pulled over by a cop, who smells alcohol on the priest's breath and spots the empty wine bottle on the floor of the car. The cop asks the priest, "Father, have you been drinking tonight?"

"No sir, nothing but water," says the priest.

The trooper says, "Then why do I smell wine?"

The priest thinks for a moment and exclaims, "Good Lord! He's done it again!"

"St. Patrick—one of the few saints whose feast day presents the opportunity to get determinedly whacked and make a fool of oneself all under the guise of acting Irish."

—CHARLES M. MADIGAN

Why is it difficult to borrow money from a leprechaun?
Because he's always a little short.

Two friends are talking on the day after St. Patrick's Day. "I had a crazy night," the first friend says. "I got really drunk at the bar and, you're never going to believe this, I took a bus home."

"How's that a big deal?" his friend asks.

"Well," the first friend explains, "up until yesterday I'd never driven a bus before."

Why doesn't a woman ever want to get engaged on St. Patrick's Day? *She doesn't want to get a sham rock.*

A small-business owner is distraught when two new big-box stores, carrying the exact same products as his store, open on either side of his business. To make matters worse, the store on his left puts a sign on its building that reads *Best Black Friday Deals*. The competitor on his right hangs an even larger sign that reads *Lowest Black Friday Prices Around*. The small-business owner panics until he gets a brilliant idea. He puts a sign, larger than both, above the door of his store that reads *Black Friday Deals—Main Entrance*.

"Every year, Christmas gets longer and longer, and you don't care, do you? Every year, you just take more of the calendar for yourself. How long does it take you people to shop? It's beyond belief! It's insane! When I was a kid, Halloween was Halloween, and Santa wasn't poking his nose into it!"—LEWIS BLACK

Why do turkeys gobble? *Because they never learned table manners.*

———◆———

What's a Thanksgiving turkey's favorite type of doll? *Gobble-heads.*

———◆———

Why is soup on Thanksgiving always more expensive? *It's got a ton of carrots.*

———◆———

If Pilgrims were alive today, what would they be most famous for? *Their age.*

What holiday do vampires celebrate every November? *Fangs-giving.*

> "I celebrated Thanksgiving in an old-fashioned way. I invited everyone in my neighborhood to my house, we had an enormous feast, and then I killed them and took their land."—JON STEWART

What happened to the Easter Bunny who misbehaved in school? *He was immediately eggspelled.*

Why do people paint Easter eggs? *It's much easier than wallpapering them.*

A parishioner who only attends church on holidays is leaving church after Easter mass. The preacher is standing at the door to shake hands. He grabs the parishioner by the hand and pulls him aside. "You need to join the Army of the Lord!" the pastor tells the parishioner.

The parishioner replies, "I'm already in the Army of the Lord, pastor."

The pastor questions, "Then how come I don't see you in church except at Christmas and Easter?"

The parishioner whispers, "I'm in the secret service."

"Happy Easter everyone! Jesus dies, comes back from the dead—and we get chocolate eggs. It's like turn-down service from God."

—DENIS LEARY

A young boy is sitting in his grandmother's kitchen, watching her prepare Thanksgiving dinner. "What are you doing to the turkey?" the boy asks his grandmother. "Oh, I'm just stuffing the bird," his grandmother replies. "Wow, that's cool," the boy remarks. "Are you going to hang it in the living room next to the deer head?"

A woman is looking for a Thanksgiving turkey, but can't find a bird big enough to feed her massive family. She asks the stock boy, "Do these turkeys get any bigger?" The stock boy replies, "No, they've stopped growing, ma'am. Those turkeys are dead."

What should you do the moment you realize your house is surrounded by zombies? *Pray that it's Halloween.*

Why was the student vampire tired in the morning? *Because he was up all night studying for his blood test!*

How did the ghost say goodbye to the vampire? *"So long, sucker!"*

What's the problem with jogging on New Year's Eve? *The ice falls out of your drink!*

———•••———

What do you call always having a date for New Year's Eve? *Social security.*

"The proper behavior all through the holiday season is to be drunk. This drunkenness culminates on New Year's Eve, when you get so drunk you kiss the person you're married to."—P.J. O'ROURKE

At a New Year's Eve party, a woman stands up on the bar and announces that it is almost midnight. She says that at midnight, she wants every husband to stand next to the one person who makes his life worth living. As the clock strikes twelve, the bartender is almost crushed to death.

Chapter 4

WORKING IT:

Jokes for the office and every profession

Since many people spend more time at work and with coworkers than with their own family, it's a great idea to have a few office-related jokes up your sleeve to break the ice with people you don't know very well. These jokes will be sure to have 'em smiling all the way from the water cooler to the cubicle.

A man shows up for work with his arm in a cast.

"What happened to you?" his assistant asks.

"I broke my arm in two places yesterday."

"Man, that sucks," says his assistant. "It would probably be a good idea to avoid those two places from now on."

The head of human resources is interviewing a potential candidate for the open position of corporate attorney. "Would you consider yourself an honest lawyer?" the HR person asks in the interview.

"Honest?" the lawyer responds. "Let me tell you how honest I am. My father sold everything he had to put me through law school. After my very first case, I paid him back in full."

"That's very impressive," the HR person admits. "What was the case?"

The attorney fidgets in his seat and says, "He sued me for the money."

A man is begging a judge to let him off jury duty because of his job. "I'm sure your company can get along fine without you for a few days," the judge tells the man.

"I know," the man answers. "But that's what I'm trying to prevent them from figuring out."

———◆———

A man goes on a job interview. The interviewer tells him that they are looking to hire someone who is responsible. "Well, I'm your man," the applicant replies. "At my last job, whenever anything went wrong, they said I was responsible."

———◆———

"Bill," a sad-faced man says to his coworker, "I just heard the news about your uncle falling off that cliff. I'm terribly sorry. Were the two of you close?"

"We were just close enough for me to push him," Bill replies.

———◆———

An office manager is interviewing an applicant. He asks the woman if she has any unusual talents. She says she'd actually won a few national crossword puzzle contests. "Sounds good," the office manager replies, "but we want someone who will be just as intelligent during office hours."

"Oh," says the applicant. "That's good because that's when I do most of my puzzles."

———◆———

A boss shows one of his employees his new sports car. "That is amazing," the employee responds.

"Isn't it?" replies the boss. "And if you set your goals higher and work even harder this year, I can get an even better car next year."

———————

Why was the limbo dancer shocked when his wallet was stolen right out of his back pocket? *Because he didn't think anyone could stoop so low.*

———————

A struggling artist stops by the studio where his recent work is hanging for sale. The owner tells him he has good news and bad news.

"The good news is that a man dropped by the studio today and put in an offer to buy every single piece. He just wanted my guarantee that the works would be worth twice what he paid if you were to pass away. I told him they would double, possibly triple, in value. So he bought them all."

"Whoa!" exclaims the artist. "That's fantastic. What could be the bad news?"

"The guy is your doctor," the owner says.

A waiter returns to the table to ask the customer how his meal is so far. "How did you find your steak?" the waiter asks.

"I just pushed a ton of mashed potatoes to the side and there it was," said the man.

"The trouble with unemployment is that the minute you wake up in the morning you're on the job."—SLAPPY WHITE

"This brand-new laptop will do half your job for you," the IT guy explains to the senior vice president of the company.

"Perfect," the vice president replies. "Can I get two then?"

On the last mission to the moon, NASA set up a restaurant. It didn't last very long. The food was good, but there was no atmosphere.

What did the Zen Buddhist say to the hot-dog vendor?
Make me one with everything.

A man is standing on a busy street corner with a placard over his chest for the local McDonald's. On the front, in big bold letters, are the words *Free Big Mac*. A homeless man stumbles over and asks the man, "What is Mac serving time for?"

A dumb guy calls to yell at the pizza man at his local shop. "I got this pizza delivered and I specifically asked to have the pie cut into six slices. This pie is cut in eight slices!"

"What's the big deal?" the pizza man wondered.

"There is no way I'll be able to eat all these!" the man yelled.

What's Forrest Gump's e-mail password at work? *1forrest1*

A customer asks to see the manager of the restaurant where he's eating dinner. "This place is filthy," the man says to the manager.

"That's outrageous!" exclaims the manager. "You could eat your dinner off our dining room floor!"

"That's my issue," says the customer. "It looks like someone already has."

"Work is the curse of the drinking classes."
—OSCAR WILDE

Three insurance salesmen are having drinks and boasting about each company's service. The first one says, "When one of our insured died suddenly on Monday, we got the news that evening and were able to process the claim for the wife and mailed a check on Wednesday evening."

The second one says, "When one of our insured died without warning on Monday, we learned of it in two hours and were able to hand-deliver a check the same evening."

The last salesman says, "That's nothing. Our office is on the twentieth floor in the Sears Tower. One of our insured, who was washing a window on the eighty-fifth floor, slipped and fell. We handed him his check as he passed our floor."

"Hard work never killed anybody, but why take a chance?"—CHARLIE MCCARTHY

A salesman is peddling his goods from door to door in a massive high-rise building. He knocks at a young man's apartment and asks him, "Would you like to buy a top-of-the-line toothbrush? It's only ten dollars."

"Ten bucks for a toothbrush!" the man yells. "What moron would pay ten dollars for a toothbrush? You're out of your mind."

"All right then," the salesman continues, "then how about a fresh-baked brownie for a dollar?" The man thinks it over and says, "Okay, why not?"

The salesman hands over the brownie. The man takes a bite and spits it out onto the floor in the hallway.

"My god, that tastes like crap!" he yells.

"Well, that's because it is crap," the salesman explains. "So can I interest you in a toothbrush?"

"I'll take some pork chops," the woman tells the butcher, "and make them lean."

"No problem," the butcher replies. "Which way?"

A music store was robbed last week. The robbers made off with the lute.

"If a man smiles all the time, he's probably selling something that doesn't work."

—GEORGE CARLIN

A young man walks into a record store and asks the clerk, "Do you have anything by the Doors?"

"Sure," replies the clerk, "a mop bucket and a fire extinguisher."

———————

A man goes back to a bookstore to complain about a recent purchase. "I bought this book last week called *The Biggest Cowards in History*, but the minute I opened the book, all of the pages fell out." The sales clerk looks at the book and explains, "Well, that's because it's got no spine."

Did you hear about the woman who was robbed by an unemployed acupuncturist? *She was stabbed more than 167 times, but she felt awesome the next day.*

Why did the masseuse have to close up his shop? *He kept rubbing people the wrong way.*

A store manager watches from a distance as a salesperson argues with a customer. After a few minutes, the customer storms out of the store.

"I saw what just happened," the manager says, "and I guess you've forgotten my motto of 'the customer is always right.'"

"I know," the salesperson says, "but . . ."

"No buts," says the manager. "The customer is always right."

"Fine," responds the salesperson.

"What were you two arguing about?" the manager asks.

The salesperson answers, "He called you an idiot."

A man walks into a pet store, interested in a parrot. He notices a gorgeous bird with a red ribbon on its right ankle and a blue ribbon on the left ankle. The man asks the store owner about the ribbons.

"Oh, this is a specially trained parrot. If you tug on the red ribbon, the parrot will recite the Declaration of Independence. If you tug on the blue ribbon, he recites the Gettysburg Address."

"That's pretty awesome," the man responds, "but what happens if you tug both at the same time?"

The parrot answers the man, "I'd fall off my perch, you moron."

"I live in a two-income household . . . but who knows how long my mom can keep that up."

—SHMUEL BREBAN

A taxi passenger tapped the driver on the shoulder to ask him a question about the city. The driver screams, loses control of the car, nearly hits a bus, drives up on the sidewalk, and stops the car inches before it crashes through the front of a store window. Both men sit completely silent until the driver turns and says, "Look man, don't *ever* do that to me again. You scared the crap out of me!"

The passenger apologizes and says, "I didn't realize that a little tap would scare you so much."

The driver replies, "Sorry, it's not really your fault. Today is my first day as a cab driver. Before this I drove a hearse."

———◆———

An admiral is staring off the deck of his battleship at the approaching enemy on the horizon.

"Fetch my red shirt," the admiral says to his first officer. "If I'm wounded in battle, I don't want the men to see I'm bleeding. It will kill morale."

"But sir," says the first officer, "there is a fleet of fifteen ships coming right for us."

"Oh," the admiral sighs. "Well, in that case go grab my brown pants."

"Employees make the best dates; you don't have to pick them up and they're always tax-deductible."—ANDY WARHOL

A heartless drill instructor screamed at his platoon for over an hour. He got in the face of a private and yelled, "I bet when I die you'll show up at my grave and spit on it!"

"Not me," the private said. "After I get out of the army I'm never standing in a line again."

—◆—

A cop pulls over a woman going the wrong way down a one-way street.

"Where the heck do you think you're going?" the cop asks.

"I don't know, but I must be late because it looks like everyone is coming back."

"Farming looks easy when your plow is a pencil and you're a thousand miles from a cornfield."—DWIGHT D. EISENHOWER

Did you hear about the woman who tried to make a career out of being a gold digger? *It didn't really pan out.*

—◆—

Did you hear about the man who got a job as a human cannonball? *He was so excited he went ballistic.*

How did the circus owner get so rich? *He spent years paying his employees peanuts.*

Why is it so hard for dwarves to get work? *Employers don't like paying people under the table.*

Did you hear about the family that was so poor that a burglar broke into their home and all he got was practice?

"There's a pizza place near where I live
that sells only slices . . . in the back you
can see a guy tossing a triangle in the air."

—STEVEN WRIGHT

A church puts an ad in the newspaper for a person to ring the bell in the belfry on Sunday mornings. No one applies for the position except for a young man with no arms. The church administrator isn't sure he can handle the job, but the man climbs the tower and rings the bell using just his head. On his first Sunday on the job, the man gets a little too excited and hits the bell a little too hard with his melon. He falls from the belfry and lands on the church steps. Two parishioners late for services rush past him.

"Who was that guy?" the wife asks her husband as they enter the church.

"I'm not sure," the husband replies, "but his face does ring a bell."

Why did the weatherman take a leave of absence after breaking both arms and both legs? *He would have trouble working with the four casts.*

"I used to be a mime . . . but now I can talk about it . . . "—STEWART FRANCIS

A college professor was very worried about his recent study on earthquakes. It turns out his findings were on shaky ground.

———◆———

Elias Howe is credited with being the inventor of the zipper, but most of his friends called him the lord of the flies.

———◆———

Why are photographers always so depressed? *Because they don't do anything all day but focus on the negatives.*

"I always wanted to be somebody, but now I realize I should have been more specific."
—LILY TOMLIN

A man goes to get his haircut and the barber asks, "Should I cut the hair in back?"

The man replies, "What's wrong with doing it right here in the chair?"

———◆———

Did you hear that everyone at the mint went on strike?
They wanted to make less money.

What did one geologist say to the other while they both stared down at a giant fissure in the rocks? *"I wonder whose fault this is."*

A woman is amazed by pastor who lives next door and how quickly he changes his personality. Around the neighborhood, he is incredibly shy, quiet, and timid. As soon as he begins to preach, he becomes loud, boisterous, and is able to entertain the congregation with his sermons.

"I'm not sure how you go from one personality to the next," the woman tells the pastor over coffee.

"Oh, it's simple," the pastor explains. "That guy in church is my altar ego."

Who is constantly bossing around the office supplies?
The ruler.

A construction worker accidentally cuts off one of his ears with an electric saw. He calls out to a guy walking on the street below, "Hey, do you see my ear down there?"

The guy on the street picks up an ear. "Is this it?"

"No," replies the construction worker, "mine had a pencil behind it."

Two factory workers are talking. The woman says, "I can make the boss give me the day off."

The man asks, "And how would you do that?"

The woman says, "Just wait and see."

She then hangs upside down from the ceiling.

The boss comes in and asks, "What are you doing?"

The woman replies, "I'm a light bulb."

The boss then says, "You've been working so much that you've gone crazy. I think you need to take the day off."

The man starts to follow her and the boss says, "Where are you going?"

The man says, "I'm going home, too. How am I supposed to work in the dark?"

A young man is fired from his job after asking customers if they wanted "smoking or nonsmoking." He was fired because the correct terminology in the funeral home business is "cremation or burial."

Unable to read the name on the label of a package, a postman decides that the weight of the box and the words left on the ripped label mean the package is for the local book shop. "I've got a package that I think is for you," the mailman tells the store owner.

"Well, what's the name on the label?" the store owner asks.

"That's the problem. It's obliterated."

"Well, it can't be for me," the store owner answers. "My name is John."

"I'll never forget the time they gave me a farewell party at work. I was so surprised—I didn't even know I was fired."—PAUL DILLERY

A tour guide is leading a group through a museum in London. "This mummy here is over 5,000 years old," the guide told the group. "It's possible that Moses saw it."

A tourist raises her hand and asks, "When was Moses ever in London?"

"No man goes before his time . . . unless the boss leaves early."—GROUCHO MARX

Two painters paint a house and hand the customer the bill. The customer notices that the men charged no money for the actual paint. The customer says, "You guys did such a good job. Why aren't you charging me for the paint?"

The head painter looks at the man and says, "Don't worry about the paint, it's on the house."

———◆———

Did you hear about the painter who kept getting fired for dropping things on people? *He couldn't hold his lacquer.*

———◆———

Did you hear about the farmer who won an award from the U.S. Department of Agriculture? *He was outstanding in his field.*

———◆———

Old bankers never die, they just lose interest.

———◆———

A client receives his bill from his lawyer in the mail. He's livid at the amount and calls the lawyer to berate him for charging such ridiculous fees. The lawyer listens for a moment before stopping the client midsentence.

"You know," the lawyer says, "you're being a real jerk about this and I'm beginning to regret naming my first boat after you."

———◆———

A very successful lawyer buys a new Ferrari. He parks in front of his office, ready to show it off to his colleagues. As he gets out, a truck passes too close and completely tears the door off of the driver's side. The counselor immediately grabs his cell phone, dials 911, and within minutes a policeman pulls up to take a report. Before the officer has a chance to ask any questions, the lawyer starts screaming hysterically. His Ferrari, which he had just picked up the day before, was now completely ruined and would never be the same, no matter what the body shop did to it. When the lawyer finally winds down from his ranting and raving, the officer shakes his head in disgust.

"I can't believe how materialistic you lawyers are," he says. "All you care about is money and your possessions."

The lawyer unleashes a stream of obscenities before the officer can calm him down. "Hear me out . . . see, you are so worried about your car, you didn't even notice that the accident took off your left arm."

"Oh my god!" screams the lawyer. "Where's my Rolex?"

Chapter 5

AMERICA'S GREATEST COMEDIANS:

Jokes about politicians and history

roucho Marx, an American comedian, once said, "Politics is the art of looking for trouble, finding it everywhere, diagnosing it incorrectly, and applying the wrong remedies." Marx may have been from another time, but his words still ring true today. Every year it seems the political scene in America gets a little more laughable. So since there is little you can do to change the world of politics, you might as well have a laugh at the men and women in charge.

How many government workers does it take to change a light bulb? *Two: one to insist the light bulb has been taken care of and the other to screw it into a faucet.*

It's only natural that all politicians have a God complex. They haven't done anything in ages, they give all the best jobs to their immediate family, and no one really believes in them.

A top official in the Democratic Party leaves his office to check out a local Republican rally. While he's spying from afar, a mugger approaches and holds him up at gunpoint. He returns to his office, upset and despondent over what happened. He explains the entire story to his assistant.

"Weren't there cops around?" the assistant asks.

"Of course," the Democrat replies.

"Well then, why didn't you yell out for help?" the assistant asks.

"What?" he shoots back, "and have Republicans think I was cheering for them?"

"You can lead a man to Congress, but you can't make him think."—MILTON BERLE

The president was awakened in the middle of the night by a call from the Pentagon.

"Mr. President," the four-star general began, "I've got good news and bad news."

"What's the bad news?" the president asked.

"The country is being taken over by aliens from another planet." "My God," the president said. "What's the good news?" "The good news is," said the general, "they pee oil and they've eaten Rush Limbaugh."

A tour guide is leading a group around the Washington, D.C., area when they come to a spot on the Potomac River.

"This is where George Washington allegedly threw a dollar across the river," the guide tells the group.

"That's impossible," says one skeptical tourist. "No one could ever throw a dollar that far."

The guide tells the man, "Well, you have to keep in mind that money went a lot farther in those days."

"Political speeches are like steer horns: a point here, a point there, and a lot of bull in between."—ALFRED E. NEUMAN

On his deathbed, a lifelong Republican told his best friend that he was switching parties and becoming a Democrat.

"My God," his friend replied, "why would you do such a thing?"

"Simple," the man muttered in his last breath, "because I'd rather one of them die than one of us."

A local congressman was sitting in his office when the phone rang. He picked it up, said little, smiled widely, said "Thank you," and hung up the phone.

He picked the phone back up to call his mother. "Mom, it's me," he said. "I won the election!"

"Honestly?" she said in response to the news.

"Does it really matter how I did it?" he replied.

"The reason there are two senators for each state is so that one can be the designated driver."—JAY LENO

Why don't politicians listen to their conscience? *They don't like taking advice from complete strangers.*

Flying across the country in Air Force One, the president jokes with his staff.

"I'm thinking about tossing a $100 bill out the window and making someone very happy."

A White House aide comments, "Why don't you throw twenty $100 bills out the window and make twenty people happy?"

Another staffer jokes, "Why don't you throw a hundred $100 bills out the window and make a hundred people happy?"

A member of the plane staff, wanting to get in on the act, chimes in and says, "Why don't you throw yourself out the window and make half the country happy?"

Two presidential aides are having coffee in a back room at the White House. "Sometimes I wish we worked for the pope and not the president," one of them says.

"Why?" asks the second aide.

"Because then we'd only have to kiss his ring."

"It's not that I disagree with Bush's economic policy or his foreign policy, it's that I believe he was a child of Satan sent here to destroy the planet Earth."—BILL HICKS

While waiting for a White House press conference to begin, a journalist turns to the stranger to his right and asks, "Did you hear the latest joke about the president?"

"Before you continue," says the stranger, "I should tell you I'm part of the White House staff."

"Okay, thanks," the journalist responds. "Then I'll tell the joke a little slower than normal."

Laura Bush tells George W. Bush, "We have this weekend free. What should we do?"

"Well, let's think," he responds.

Laura replies, "No, let's do something we both can do."

Plenty of Americans don't trust Barack Obama because they claim he's not a "real American" like they are. They have a point; they aren't like him. He's too thin.

How many politicians does it take to change a light bulb?
Two—one to change the light bulb and then one to change it back again after he gets elected.

A Republican, a Democrat, and Bill Clinton are traveling in a car when a tornado picks up the car and tosses them miles into the air. When the car finally comes back down, the three men realize they've been transported to Oz.

"I'm going to ask the Wizard for a brain," says the Democrat.

"I'm going to ask him for a heart," says the Republican.

Bill Clinton looks around and asks the two men, "Where do you think Dorothy is?"

"Schwarzenegger confesses to fathering baby with house staff member, but explains that child is destined to bring down SkyNet in 2031."—GEORGE TAKEI

Two politicians are having lunch. The first politician says, "There are many ways of making money, but there is only one honest way."

"And how's that?" the second politician asks.

The first politician laughs and replies, "I have no idea. I thought maybe you would."

• • •

Did you hear that the George W. Bush Presidential Library burned to the ground in a fire? Unfortunately, all three books were lost, and one of them was barely all colored in.

> ## "I don't know a lot about politics, but I can recognize a good party man when I see one."
> ### —MAE WEST

Richard Nixon, Jimmy Carter, and Bill Clinton are among the passengers on a boat that's about to sink. As the ship begins to capsize, Carter yells, "Quick, save the women and children!"

Nixon replies, "Screw the women!"

Clinton wonders out loud, "Do we have time for that?"

• • •

A man and his wife are discussing what they think their son will be when he grows up.

"I have an idea," says the father. He puts a ten-dollar bill, a bottle of whiskey, and a Bible on the coffee table. "If he takes the money, he'll be a banker. If he takes the whiskey, he'll be a wino, and if he takes the Bible, that means he'll be a preacher."

So the man and his wife hide just before their son comes in the door, and watch from where they're hiding. The boy saunters over to the coffee table. He picks up the ten-dollar bill, looks at it, then sets it down. He picks up the bottle of whiskey, uncorks it, sniffs it, then sets it down. He picks up the Bible, leafs through it, and sets it down. Then the boy takes the money and stuffs it into his pocket, grabs the whiskey, and walks off with the Bible under his arm.

"Well, how do you like that!" exclaims the father. "He's going to be a politician!"

———◆———

A thief sticks a gun into a man's ribs and says, "Give me your money, now!"

The man, shocked by the sudden attack, replies, "You can't do this to me. I'm a congressman!"

The thief replies, "Oh, well in that case, give me *my* money!"

"It's so cold here in Washington, D.C., that politicians have their hands in their own pockets."—BOB HOPE

Why did George Washington have trouble sleeping? *Because he found it impossible to lie.*

How many politicians does it take to screw in a light bulb? *One, but boy does it get screwed good.*

What happens when you mate a pig with a politician? *Nothing, because there are some things even a pig won't do.*

Bill and Hillary are fast asleep in the First Bedroom, when Hillary wakes and starts shaking Bill. Bill groggily opens his eyes and says, "Honey, it's 3 A.M. What do you want?"

"I have to use the bathroom," Hillary replies.

Bill responds, "Please tell me you didn't wake me up just to tell me you have to go to the bathroom."

"No," Hillary says. "I just wanted to tell you to save my spot."

"Everything is changing. People are taking their comedians seriously and the politicians as a joke."—WILL ROGERS

Why were the early days of history called the Dark Ages? *Because there were so many knights.*

———•———

Which English king invented the fireplace? *Alfred the Grate.*

———•———

How was the Roman Empire cut in half? *With a pair of Caesars.*

What kind of lighting did Noah use for the ark? *Floodlights and ark lights.*

A member of the Senate, known for his hot temper, explodes one day in mid-session and begins to shout, "Half of this Senate is made up of cowards and corrupt politicians!" All the other senators demand that the angry member withdraw his statement or be removed for the remainder of the session. After a moment to think, the angry senator apologizes. "I'm sorry," he says. "What I meant to say was half of this Senate is *not* made up of cowards and corrupt politicians!"

Two young boys are talking before school.

"My uncle ran for Senate last year," the first boy says to his classmate.

"Really?" the second boy asks. "What does he do now?"

"Nothing," the first boy explains. "He got elected."

How do you keep Vice President Joe Biden busy until lunch? *Tell him to stand in the corner of the Oval Office.*

"For most of history, Anonymous was a woman."—VIRGINIA WOOLF

Who is the most powerful individual in Washington, D.C.? *The president's dog—he can get the president to kneel in front of him.*

Why should all former senators be buried 100 feet deep when they die? *Because deep down, they're really good people.*

How did George Washington speak to his army? *In general terms.*

What are the ingredients for the homemade Bill Clinton stew? *One wiener, one cooked goose, lots of spilled beans, and tons of hot water.*

Before his inauguration, George W. Bush was invited to take a tour of the White House. After drinking several glasses of water, he asked President Clinton if he could use the bathroom in the Oval Office. He was astonished to see that the president had a solid gold urinal installed. That night, George W. told his wife, Laura, about the urinal.

"Just think," he said, "when I'm president, I'll have my own personal gold urinal!"

Laura had lunch with Hillary Clinton on her tour of the White House and told her how impressed George had been with his discovery of the president's private bathroom and gold urinal.

"Bill doesn't have a gold urinal," Hillary told Laura, "but that explains who peed in Bill's saxophone."

Hillary Clinton goes in for her annual gynecological exam. The doctor tells her she's pregnant. Hillary storms out of the office and calls Bill.

"You got me pregnant! How could you be so careless?"

After a moment of stunned silence, Bill asks, "Who is this?"

"You should be ashamed," a father tells his young son. "When Abraham Lincoln was your age, he used to walk ten miles every day to get to school."

"Really?" the son responds. "Well, when he was your age, he was president."

In an American history discussion group, a professor is trying to explain how society's idea of beauty changes with time. "For example," he says, "the winner of the Miss America pageant in 1921 stood five foot one, weighed only 108 pounds, and had measurements of 30-25-32. How do you think she'd do in today's version of the contest?"

The class was silent until one woman comments, "She'd lose for sure."

"Why is that?" asks the professor.

"Well for one thing," the student answers, "she's probably dead."

"It's a very good historical book about history."—DAN QUAYLE

A reporter corners George W. Bush at a press conference after his election. "Many people feel the only reason you were elected president is because of the enormous power and influence of your father."

"That notion is ridiculous!" says Bush. "It doesn't matter how powerful the man is. He was only allowed to vote once!"

If "pros" are opposite of "cons," does that mean "congress" is the opposite of "progress"?

President George Bush walks into the Oval Office and sees Vice President Dan Quayle celebrating wildly.

"What's going on, Mr. Quayle?" the president inquires.

"I just done finished a jigsaw puzzle in record time!" the vice president beams.

"How long did it take you?" President Bush asks.

"I did it in just over a month," Quayle explains, "but the box said it would take 3–5 years!"

"After you've heard two eyewitness accounts of an automobile accident, you begin to worry about history."—TIM ALLEN

A history teacher is discussing George Washington with his class. "George Washington not only chopped down his father's cherry tree," the teacher explains, "but also admitted to doing it. Does anyone know why his father didn't punish him?"

A girl in the front of the class answers, "Maybe because George still had the axe in his hand?"

Why's Richard Nixon like an old collector's item? *Both are worth more in the box.*

A man is sitting at a bar during a costume party when a friend comes up to him and says, "You were supposed to dress up like something that symbolized your love life."

"I am," the man says.

"You look like Abe Lincoln," the friend responds.

"Yup," he replies, taking a sip of beer. "My last four scores were seven years ago."

One night, George W. Bush is awakened by George Washington's ghost in the White House. President Bush asks him, "George, what is the best thing I could do to help the country?"

"Set an honest and honorable example, just as I did," Washington advises.

The next night, the ghost of Thomas Jefferson appears in the Oval Office.

"Tom," Bush asks, "what is the best thing I could do to help the country?"

Jefferson advises Bush, "Cut taxes and reduce the size of government."

Bush stays awake the next night and Abraham Lincoln's ghost appears.

"Abe," Bush says, "What is the best thing I could do to help the country?"

Honest Abe answers, "Take the night off and go see a play."

"He who warned, uh, the British that they weren't gonna be takin' away our arms, uh, by ringing those bells, and um, makin' sure as he's riding his horse through town to send those warning shots and bells that we were going to be sure and we were going to be free, and we were going to be armed."

—SARAH PALIN

President Obama goes to visit the Queen of England. As Air Force One arrives at Heathrow Airport, President Obama is warmly welcomed by the Queen. They are driven in a car to the edge of central London, where they get into a magnificent seventeenth-century carriage hitched to six white horses. They continue on toward Buckingham Palace and wave to the crowds gathered to greet them. Suddenly the right rear horse lets out the loudest fart ever heard in the British Empire. The smell is awful and both passengers put handkerchiefs over their noses. The two dignitaries of state do their best to ignore the incident. Because the smell lingers, the Queen feels she must say something. She turns to President Obama and says, "Mr. President, please accept my regrets. I am sure you understand there are some things that even a Queen cannot control."

Obama looks at her and replies, "Your Majesty, I completely understand. Until you mentioned it, I thought it was one of the horses."

Did you hear the rumor that the president was poisoned last week but doctors were able to find a cure? *The information is purely antidotal.*

Chapter 6

PLAYING
THE FIELD:

Jokes about sports and celebrity culture

From Tiger Woods to the Kardashians, the world of sports and celebrity is rife with perfect joking material. Though celebs are entertaining for us regular folks, it's the eccentric characters and personalities just slightly off center that keeps us coming back for more. Don't feel bad poking fun at them; they're laughing all the way to the bank! So cash in on some of the fun with these jabs at the crazy world of the rich and famous.

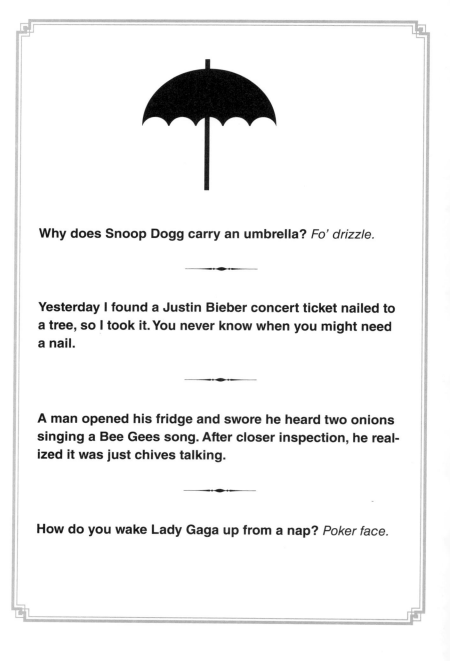

Why does Snoop Dogg carry an umbrella? *Fo' drizzle.*

Yesterday I found a Justin Bieber concert ticket nailed to a tree, so I took it. You never know when you might need a nail.

A man opened his fridge and swore he heard two onions singing a Bee Gees song. After closer inspection, he realized it was just chives talking.

How do you wake Lady Gaga up from a nap? *Poker face.*

If God is love, and love is blind, then doesn't that make Stevie Wonder God?

Kanye West compares himself to Michelangelo, Picasso, Walt Disney, and Steve Jobs. Apparently none of them could sing, either.

"Hollywood is a place where they'll pay you a thousand dollars for a kiss and fifty cents for your soul."—MARILYN MONROE

Did you know Dolly Parton was once a schoolteacher? *She loved the kids, but her biggest problem was after she wrote something on the blackboard, she'd turn around and accidentally wipe it off.*

How did Michael Jackson pick his nose? *Usually from a catalog.*

A woman is reading the newspaper while her husband is watching television next to her on the couch. Suddenly, she bursts out laughing.

"Listen to this story," she says. "A man put out a classified ad and he's offering to swap his wife for season tickets to the Red Sox."

"Wow," her husband says, not looking away from the television.

She begins to tease him and asks, "Would you swap me for season tickets?"

"Absolutely not," he answers without giving it a second thought.

"How sweet," she says, hugging him close.

"I mean," he continues, "the season is almost half over now."

Did you hear the bad news about the Sylvester Stallone marathon? *It got off to a* Rocky *start.*

A woman is eating lunch at a Los Angeles restaurant when she bumps into her favorite movie star in the ladies' room. Constantly in trouble with drugs and the police, the star mentions to the fan that she was already writing her memoir. "Some of these stories are so crazy," she admits, "the publisher is considering holding the book until I pass away."

"Wow," the fan replies, "so I guess it will be on shelves in a couple months?"

A young actor calls his agent from the set of his first film. He is playing the lead role for the first time in his career.

"How's it going?" the agent asks.

"It's amazing!" the actor gushes. "The director told me that my performance is making him consider making two films with me."

"Two?" the agent replies.

"Yeah," the actor says, "my first and my last."

"You know, let's put it this way, if all the people in Hollywood who have had plastic surgery, if they went on vacation, there wouldn't be a person left in town."—MICHAEL JACKSON

At the movie theater, a girl returning to her seat taps the shoulder of the man in the last seat in the row.

"Excuse me," she says, "but did I step on your toe on the way to the bathroom?"

"As a matter of fact, you did," says the man, expecting an apology.

"Oh good," says the girl, "then this is my row."

After a day of entertaining the troops, the Dallas Cowboys cheerleaders meet with the base commander to discuss the rest of the evening.

"Would you girls like to mess with the enlisted men or the officers this evening?" the commander asks.

"I don't think it matters to the ladies," the head cheerleader says, "but I'm sure a lot of the girls would like to get something to eat first."

Did you hear about the tragedy involving the U.S. Synchronized Swimming Team? *The captain had a heart attack in the water and drowned and the rest of team really didn't have a choice.*

———◆———

A retired boxer goes to see his doctor because he's having trouble sleeping. "Have you tried counting sheep?" the doctor asks.

"I tried," the boxer explains, "but every time I get to the number nine I stand up."

———◆———

A soccer hooligan appears before a judge. He is charged with disorderly conduct and assault after a match. The arresting officer states that the accused had thrown something into the river not far from the stadium.

"What exactly did the accused throw into the river?" the judge asks.

"Stones, sir," the officer replies.

The judge is confused. "Well, that's hardly an offense, officer."

"It was in this case, sir," the officer explains. "Stones was the name of the referee."

"Golf is a good walk spoiled."—MARK TWAIN

A frantic father calls the family doctor on the phone. "Doc, you've got to come quick! My three-year-old son just swallowed all of my golf tees."

"All right, stay calm," the doctor tells the father. "I'll be over in ten minutes."

"What should I do in the meantime?" the father asks.

The doctor answers, "I guess you could practice your putting."

"It's just a job. Grass grows, birds fly, waves pound the sand. I beat people up."—MUHAMMAD ALI

Todd took a week off from the office. He booked a vacation to go skiing. Before his first trip down the mountain, he heard an unbelievable rumble, and before he could move he was covered in snow. He found shelter in a small cave and was able to start a fire and make himself comfortable until help arrived. After a few hours, there was a digging at the front of the cave.

"Who's there?" Todd called out from inside the cave.

"Hello!" a voice called. "It's the Red Cross!"

"Beat it!" Todd yelled back. "I already donated twice this year."

"I went to a fight the other night, and a hockey game broke out."—RODNEY DANGERFIELD

The owner of a racehorse is angry because the horse he paid so much money for has yet to win a race.

"Listen to me," the man says, grabbing the horse by the harness. "You'd better win this race or you'll be working the farm tomorrow."

The horses line up in the gates, the starting gun sounds, and the gate is removed. All of the horses take off for the finish line, except the owner's horse. He is fast asleep in his starting pen.

"What the heck do you think you're doing?" the owner yells at the horse.

"I'm grabbing some rest," says the horse. "I've got to work the farm early tomorrow morning."

———◆———

What time does Serena Williams go to bed? *Tennish.*

———◆———

Give a man a fish and he will eat for a day. Teach him how to fish and he will sit in a boat and drink beer all day.

———◆———

A goalkeeper hosted a celebratory dinner at his house after his team won the league championship. Before dinner, he asked the coach to say grace. The coach concluded his prayer by saying, "We ask that you bless this food in the name of the father, and of the son, and of the goalie host."

Old man Morty is telling his grandson about his days as a prize fighter. "Then there was the match against Hammerhands Callahan," Morty begins. "It was quite a bout. By the third round, I had him nervous."

"Really?" his grandson asks excitedly.

"Yup," Morty replies, "he was pretty nervous he was going to kill me."

> ## "I'm tired of hearing about money, money, money, money, money. I just want to play the game, drink Pepsi, wear Reebok."
> ### —SHAQUILLE O'NEAL

A group of chess enthusiasts check into a hotel and are standing in the lobby discussing their recent tournament victories. After about an hour, the manager comes out of the office and asks them to disperse.

"But why?" they ask, as they move off.

"Because," he said, "I can't stand chess nuts boasting in an open foyer."

The hardest part about water polo is keeping the horse from drowning.

Football is a game played by incredibly fit men who run around for three hours for the amusement of millions of out-of-shape fans.

"If a woman has to choose between catching a fly ball and saving an infant's life, she will choose to save the infant's life without even considering if there is a man on base."—DAVE BARRY

While sitting on the deck of the course bar after a round of golf, Bill is hit in the head with an errant drive. By the time the offending golfer finds him, Bill is already angry and holding an ice pack to his head.

"I'm so sorry!" the golfer says. "It just got away from me!"

"You'll be more than sorry!" Bill yells. "I'm going to sue you for $5 million for your carelessness."

"I yelled 'fore,'" the golfer explains.

"Fine," Bill answered. "I'll take four."

———◆———

A skydiving student is being instructed on how to open his chute. "You count to ten out loud," the instructor said, "and then pull the rip cord." The student asks, "W-w-w-w-w-h-h-a-t w-w-w-w-w-a-s that that that num-num-number a-a-a-gain?"

The instructor replies, "Two."

———◆———

The Olympics this year featured a representative from each of two hundred different countries. One more representative and they'll match the number in the Pitt-Jolie family.

———◆———

"There's a fine line between fishing and just standing on the shore like an idiot."
—STEVEN WRIGHT

A golfer sets his ball on the tee and lines up his shot. He takes a massive swing and puts the ball into a huge forest of trees along the fairway. He finds his ball and sees an opening he thinks he could sneak the ball through. Taking out his three wood, the golfer takes another mighty swing. The ball bounces off a tree and fires back at him, nailing him in the forehead and killing him instantly. St. Peter meets him at the pearly gates and asks how his golf game had been progressing.

The golfer said to St. Peter confidently, "Got up here in two, didn't I?"

———◆———

Two golfers are starting a round. "That's a weird-looking ball you're using. What kind is it?"

"Oh, it's awesome," the second golfer exclaims. "It's a completely unlosable ball! If it goes into the bushes, the ball lights up. If it lands in a water hazard, it floats to the surface. If it's dark out, it emits a beeping sound until you find it. The ball is sensational."

"Wow, that's amazing," says the first golfer. "Where did you get it?"

"Last time I golfed," reveals the second golfer, "I found it in the woods."

"Skiing combines outdoor fun with knocking down trees with your face."—DAVE BARRY

An old man and his wife are in bed. After lying silently for a few minutes, the old man farts and says, "Seven points."

His wife rolls over and says, "What in the heck are you talking about?"

The old man answers, "I'm playing fart football!"

A few minutes later the wife farts and says, "Touchdown! Tie score."

After about five minutes the old man farts again and says, "Touchdown! I'm winning 14 to 7!"

Furious about losing, the wife rips another fart and yells out, "The score is tied!"

The pressure is on and the old man refuses to lose. He strains incredibly hard, but instead of farting he accidentally poops the bed. The wife hears the noise and asks, "What in the world was that noise?"

The old man replies, "That's the whistle for halftime. Switch sides."

Two men go hunting in the forest. They are walking along with their guns and enjoying the outdoors when one man suddenly collapses. His friend grabs him to see what's wrong, but he won't move. He knows something is wrong and calls 911. The man shouts frantically into the phone, "My buddy just collapsed! He isn't moving and I think he's dead! What do I do?"

"Well first," the 911 operator replies calmly, "you need to make sure he is actually dead."

The operator hears the man leave the phone for a moment. She hears footsteps followed by a moment of silence and then a loud bang.

The friend returns to the phone. "Okay, he's dead, now what?"

A golfer is having a horrible day on the course. After another shot into the woods, he says aloud, "I'd move heaven and earth to break 100 on this course."

His caddy puts the club back into his bag and says, "Try just heaven, because you've already moved most of the earth."

"Wrestling is ballet with violence."
—JESSE VENTURA

A San Francisco Giants fan, a San Diego Padres fan, and a Los Angeles Dodgers fan are climbing a mountain and arguing about which one loves his team more. The Padres fan insists he's the most loyal.

"This is for San Diego!" he yells, and jumps off the side of the mountain. Not to be outdone, the Giants fan is next to profess his love for his team.

He yells, "This is for San Francisco!" and pushes the Dodgers fan off the mountain.

———◆———

Two old men are in the middle of an intense chess match. In the middle of player one's next move, player two lets out a loud sneeze.

"God bless you," player one says.

Player two snaps back, "Did you come here to talk or did you come here to play?"

———◆———

Two guys are playing golf. Two women in front of them are really taking their time and are slowing the men up.

One man says to his friend, "I'm gonna go ask those ladies if we can play through."

He starts walking, but about halfway there, he turns around. When he gets back, his friend asks what happened.

He replies, "One of those women is my wife, and the other is my mistress. Will *you* go talk to them?"

So the second man starts to walk over. He gets halfway there and turns around. When he gets back, his friend asks, "Now what happened?"

To this he replies, "Small world."

A skydiving instructor is answering questions for his beginner's class.

"So if my parachute doesn't open," a student asks, "and my reserve chute doesn't work, how long have I got until I hit the ground?"

The instructor tells the man, "You've got the rest of your life."

A rookie pitcher is struggling on the mound, so the catcher walks up to have a quick talk with him.

"I think I've figured out your problem," the catcher tells the shaky southpaw. "You always lose control at exactly the same point in every game."

The pitcher feels a little relieved, thinking he has the answer to his issue.

"When do I usually lose my control?" he asks his battery mate.

"It's usually," the catcher admits, "right after the national anthem."

"I've always been famous, it's just no one knew it yet."—LADY GAGA

After years of gambling, an unlucky gambler finally figures out the way to leave Las Vegas with a small fortune. He goes to Las Vegas with a large fortune.

What do you call a person who pretends to be a college student? *A college athlete.*

Tom and Clark are standing on the roof of their building drinking a few beers on their break when Clark says, "Hey Tom, did you know that if you jump off this building, after you get down so far, a draft will pull you back inside the building on the third floor?"

"Get outta here," says Tom.

"I'm serious. Watch me," Clark says. Clark hops off the building, and sure enough, he is taken in by the draft to the third-floor window. He takes the elevator back to the top and Tom is standing there in awe.

"I can't believe it," says Tom.

"I know. You should try it."

So Tom hops off and plunges into the ground.

A doorman working below sees Tom splat to the ground and screams back up, "Superman, you're a real jerk when you're drunk."

"Burt Reynolds once asked me out. I was in his room."—PHYLLIS DILLER

Why don't Batman and Robin go fishing anymore? *Robin always eats the worms.*

How do you find Ronald McDonald at a nude beach? *You look for the sesame seed buns!*

Did you hear O.J. Simpson is doing stand-up in jail? *He kills.*

Strip poker is the only game where the more you lose, the more you have to show for it.

Sherlock Holmes and Dr. Watson go on a camping trip. After a good meal and a bottle of wine, they lay down for the night and go to sleep. Some hours later, Holmes awakens and nudges his faithful friend. "Watson, look up at the sky and tell me what you see."

Watson replies, "I see millions and millions of stars."

"What does that tell you?" Holmes ponders for a minute.

"Astronomically, it tells me that there are millions of galaxies, and potentially billions of planets. Astrologically, I observe that Saturn is in Leo. Horologically, I deduce that the time is approximately a quarter past three. Theologically, I can see that God is all powerful and that we are small and insignificant. Meteorologically, I suspect that we will have a beautiful day tomorrow. What does it tell you?"

Holmes is silent for a minute, then says, "It tells me that someone has stolen our tent."

"Anyone who's just driven 90 yards against huge men trying to kill them has earned the right to do jazz hands."
—CRAIG FERGUSON

Chapter 7

DEATH AND TAXES:

Jokes about health, aging, and dying

There's an old saying that there are two things no one can avoid: death and taxes. While you might be able to avoid taxes for a while, there is no cheating death. It's inevitable. Luckily, old age and its ailments will make a person either forget death is coming or wish it got there sooner. In any event, these jokes prove that laughter is the best medicine.

A man goes to a doctor for his yearly routine physical. The nurse starts with the basic health questions.

"How much do you weigh?" she asks.

"Oh, about 165 pounds," he says.

The nurse puts him on the scale and his actual weight is 187.

The nurse then asks, "And how tall are you?"

"Oh, about six feet tall," he says. The nurse checks and sees that he's only five foot eight. She then takes his blood pressure and tells him it's incredibly high.

"High!" the man exclaims. "Well, what do you expect? When I came in here today I was tall and lanky. Now I'm short and fat!"

A man with a broken hand says to his doctor, "Will I be able to play guitar after the operation on my hand?"

The doctor says, "Yes, of course."

"That's great!" says the man. "I never could before."

A woman explains to her doctor her recent issues with going to the bathroom.

"I've had horrible constipation," she explains. "I haven't been able to go for weeks."

"Are you doing anything for it?" the doctor asks.

"Well, I'll force myself to sit on the toilet for a half hour in the morning and a half hour before bed."

"No, I meant are you taking anything?"

"Oh," she replies. "Yeah, I usually take a magazine."

"He's so old that when he orders a three-minute egg, they ask for the money up front."
—MILTON BERLE

A man asks his good friend if he can recommend a doctor. "Yeah," the man says, "I'll give you the number to the guy we go see. He's a family doctor. He treats mine and I support his."

"I'd go out with women my age, but there are no women my age."—GEORGE BURNS

A man visits the doctor because he's suffering from a miserable winter cold. His doctor prescribes some antibiotics, but they don't help. On his next visit, the doctor gives the man a shot, but it doesn't do any good. On his third visit, the doctor tells the man to go home and take a steaming hot bath. As soon as he gets out of the bath, he should open all of the windows in his house and stand naked in the draft.

"But doctor," the man protests, "if I do that, I'll probably get pneumonia."

"I know," says the doctor. "But at least I know how to cure pneumonia."

A woman accompanies her husband to a doctor's visit. After the checkup, the doctor calls only her into his office. "The outlook isn't good," he tells her.

"Your husband is under a tremendous amount of stress. If you don't do exactly what I tell you, he may not survive to see the end of the month. Each morning, make him a nice healthy breakfast. Do the same for lunch and dinner. Always be in a pleasant mood around him and keep his spirits up. Don't burden him with chores or stress him with the details of your day. At night, if he's up for it, agree to any request for sexual pleasure. If you do all those things, he'll live a long life." On the way home, the husband asks his wife what the doctor said to her in the closed-door meeting.

She replies, "You're going to die."

A man went to the dentist to have a cavity worked on. The dentist was on vacation so the man settled for the doctor filling in.

———◆———

A woman runs into a doctor's office and says, "Doctor! You have to help me! Everywhere I touch on my body it hurts!"

The doctor replies, "Show me." So the woman pokes her ankle and screams in pain. She pokes her knee and yells again. She pokes her forehead and screams louder than before. She is about to continue when the doctor says, "That's enough, let me think this over." He thinks for a minute and says, "I think I know what your problem is. You broke your finger."

———◆———

A worried father calls the family doctor because he thinks his teen son has caught a venereal disease.

"I think he got it from the maid," says the concerned dad, "and I've also been sleeping with the maid."

"Okay," the doctor replies calmly. "Well, when you bring him into the office we'll take a look at you as well."

"And that's not all," the father continues. "I think I might have given it to his mother."

"Oh no!" cries the doctor. "Well, now we might all have it!"

"People are saying that I'm an alcoholic, and that's not true, because I only drink when I work, and I'm a workaholic."—RON WHITE

A man goes to the dentist for his six-month exam. The man tells the dentist, "My teeth are great. I never use mouthwash, rarely brush my teeth, never floss, never use a breath mint, and eat onions and garlic with just about every meal. I also never have bad breath." The dentist agrees his teeth are decent, but he will need an operation.

"On what?" the man asks.

The dentist responds quickly, "Your nose."

———※———

Two men are roommates in a hospital. Because they are both weak from sickness, the men are unable to speak for weeks. Finally, one man says to the other, "American."

His roommate replies, "Canadian."

Another week goes by and the first man says weakly, "Danny."

The roommate can only reply, "Phil."

Another week passes and the first man mutters to his roommate, "Cancer."

His roommate replies back, "Virgo."

———※———

A patient and psychologist were meeting for the first time.

"I think I'm a goat," the patient tells the new doctor.

"All right," the doctor says as he jots notes down. "And how long have you had this feeling?"

The man told him, "Ever since I was a kid."

"Everything that used to be a sin is now a disease."—BILL MAHER

A patient in a mental hospital would spend his entire day with his ear pressed up against a wall. The doctor would watch this man, day after day, sit against the wall. The doctor finally decides to see what the patient is always listening to, so he puts his ear up to the wall and listens alongside the man. He hears nothing.

He turns to the mental patient and says, "I don't hear anything coming from the wall."

The mental patient replies, "Yeah, I know, and it's been like that for months!"

A new patient settles comfortably onto the couch and the psychiatrist begins his therapy session.

"I'm not aware of your exact problem," the doctor says, "so perhaps you should start at the very beginning."

"Of course," replies the patient. "In the beginning, I created the Heavens and the Earth . . ."

"Roses are red, violets are blue, I'm schizophrenic and so am I."
—BILL MURRAY IN *WHAT ABOUT BOB?*

Three older ladies are discussing the trials of getting older. One says, "Sometimes I catch myself with a jar of mayonnaise in my hand in front of the refrigerator and can't remember whether I need to put it away or start making a sandwich."

The second lady chimes in, "Yes, sometimes I find myself on the landing of the stairs and can't remember whether I was on my way up or on my way down."

The third one responds, "Well, I'm sure glad I don't have that problem, knock on wood." She raps her knuckles on the table, then says, "That must be the door, I'll get it."

"My mother used to say: the older you get, the better you get . . . unless you're a banana."—BETTY WHITE

Two men are sitting in a bar drinking. The first man notices two old men across the bar. He points at them and says to his friend, "That's us in about ten years."

His friend looks up, laughs, puts his head back down, and says, "That's us now, because that's a mirror."

———◆———

A middle-aged man goes to the doctor about his recent issues with memory loss.

"Doctor, I just can't seem to remember much anymore."

"Okay," the doctor said sympathetically, "it might be an issue we can get a grip on. When exactly did you begin having this issue?"

The man looks at the doctor and replies, "What issue?"

A man is standing on the scale in his bathroom and sucking in his gut. His wife catches him and says, "That's not going to help at all."

"Yes it is," the man barks. "Now I can see the numbers!"

"Nothing makes a smoker happier than to see an old person smoking."—BILL HICKS

"My grandmother has Alzheimer's," a teen tells his friend as they walked past her sitting in the living room.

"That sucks," the friend says.

"Yeah, but it's got some upside," the teen replies. "Like when I get twenty dollars for my birthday every week."

Two old men are sitting on a park bench. The first man takes a look into his friend's ear and says, "Do you know you've got a suppository stuck in your ear?"

"Really?" says the first man. "I had no idea. But I guess that explains where I put my hearing aid."

———

Two old women are discussing the disgusting habits of their husbands. "Even after all these years, my husband will not stop biting his nails," the first woman explains.

"My husband had the same habit," the second woman explained, "but I fixed that. I just hid his teeth."

———

A grandfather is walking home with his granddaughter after church. "Did God make you, PopPop?" the girl asks.

"Yep! He certainly did," the old man answers.

"And did he make me too?" she asks next.

"Of course he did," the old man answers again.

"Well," she replies, "he's certainly getting better at it."

"Do you realize you were speeding?" the officer asks the old woman after pulling her over.

"Yes, officer," she replies, embarrassed, "but I've got a very good excuse."

"What's that?" he asks.

"I'm trying to get where I'm going before I forget where I'm going."

"Middle age is when your old classmates are so grey and wrinkled and bald they don't recognize you."—BENNETT CERF

An old woman accidentally drops her fake teeth at the park while walking her dog. She can't find the teeth anywhere in the tall grass. A man spots her bending over and asks what she lost. "I dropped my false teeth somewhere around here."

"Oh," the man says, "that's no big deal. Here, try this pair on."

He hands her a set of teeth that are too big for her mouth. He hands her a second set of teeth that are too small. Finally, the third set fits just right.

"Thank you so much," the old woman says. "Do you have a business card? I've been looking for a good dentist for some time."

"Oh, I'm not a dentist," the man replies. "I'm an undertaker."

An old couple are sitting in their living room. The old woman leans over and says to the old man, "Remember when we were younger and you used to hold my hand?" The old man grabs the old woman's hand.

Then she says, "Remember when we were younger and you used to put your arm around me?" The old man puts his arm around the old woman.

Then she says, "Remember when we were younger and you used to nibble on my ear?" To the old woman's surprise, the old man gets up off the couch and starts to walk away.

"Honey, where are you going?" she asks. The old man replies, "I'm going to get my dentures."

A new man is brought into a prison cell with a cellmate who is already 100 years old. The new cellmate asks the old man his story. The old con says, "You look at me, I'm old and worn out, but if you can believe it, I used to live the life of Riley. I wintered on the Riviera, had a boat and four luxury cars, dated the most beautiful women, and I ate in all the best restaurants around the world."

The new man asks, "What happened?"

"Riley finally realized his credit cards were missing."

"If you're older, you're smarter. I just believe that. If you're in an argument with someone older than you, you should listen to them. Even if they're wrong, their wrongness is rooted in more information than you have."—LOUIS C.K.

An old man is taking the road test to renew his driver's license. The instructor tells the old man that when she taps on the dashboard she wants him to slow down and show her the action he'd take if a young child ran out in front of his car. The instructor taps the dashboard a few minutes into the ride. The old man screeches the car to a halt, puts down the window, and yells to the empty street, "Be careful where you're going, you little jerk!"

A young man passes an elderly man crying on a park bench. The young man stops and asks if everything is okay. The old man looks up with his eyes filled with tears.

"Kid," the old man says, "I'm ninety years old. Last week I married a woman half my age. She does everything for me—she cooks my meals, washes my clothes, shops for me, and will do anything I ask in the bedroom."

"Oh," replies the young man. "Well, that doesn't sound bad at all. Why are you sitting here crying?"

"Because," the old man sobs loudly, "I can't remember where the hell I live!"

An old man was fitted with brand-new hearing aids. His hearing was better than it was in his prime. He returned to the clinic a week after the fitting and the audiologist asked him, "How are your hearing aids working?"

The old man replied, "They are fantastic. They work so well I've changed my will three times since last week."

"My body is dropping so fast, my gynecologist wears a hard hat."—JOAN RIVERS

A husband and wife wake up one morning, and when the man leans over to kiss his wife, she yells in his face.

"Don't touch me! I'm dead."

"What are you talking about?" the husband asks. "We're both lying in bed. You can't be dead."

"I must be dead," the wife responds, "because I woke up this morning and nothing hurts."

Three senior citizens are sitting on a park bench complaining about their failing bodies. "Every morning, I get up at 6 A.M.," the first man explains, "and I try to pee, but nothing but a trickle comes out." The second man adds, "I get up at 6 A.M. too, and it feels like I've got to move my bowels, but I sit down on the toilet and nothing happens."

The third man chimes in the conversation and tells his friends, "I pee and move my bowels at exactly 7 A.M. every morning."

"That's not bad," the first man responds. "Why are you complaining?"

The third man admits, "The problem is I don't usually wake up until 8 A.M."

"Eat well, stay fit, die anyway."—PROVERB

An adorable old woman visits the doctor. "Doctor, I have this problem with gas, but it really doesn't bother me too much. It never smells and is always silent. As a matter of fact, I've farted at least ten times since I've been here in your office. You didn't know I was farting because it doesn't smell and is silent."

The doctor says, "I see. Take these pills and come back to see me next week."

The next week the lady returns. "Doctor," she says, "I don't know what the heck you gave me, but now my farts, although still silent, stink terribly."

"Good," the doctor says. "Now that we've cleared up your sinuses, let's work on your hearing."

Three old friends, all with very bad hearing, meet on the corner.

"Isn't it windy?" the first man asks.

"No," says the second, "it's Thursday."

"Agreed," says the third man, "let's go grab a beer."

> **"A sixty-seven-year-old woman in Spain gave birth to twins over the weekend. The mother and babies are doing fine, but the doctor who delivered the babies is still really nauseous."**—CONAN O'BRIEN

A man goes to the nursing home to visit his eighty-four-year-old father. While there he notices the nurse hand his father a cup of hot chocolate and a Viagra pill. The man asks the nurse, "Why are you doing that? At his age, what will either do for him?"

"The hot chocolate," the nurse explains, "will help him fall asleep faster."

"All right," the man replies, "and what about the Viagra?"

"That keeps him from rolling out of bed."

A wife is visiting her husband in a nursing home. He sneezes, and for the first time in his life, covers his mouth with his hand. "I'm so proud of you," his wife says. "You finally learned to put your hand in front of your mouth after all these years."

"Of course I have," her husband replies. "How else am I going to catch my teeth?"

An old man is bragging to his roommate at the nursing home about his new hearing aid. The man goes on and on about how great the hearing aid is and how well he can hear with it.

"It was also very expensive," the man says to his friend.

"Well, good for you," his friend replies. "What kind is it?"

"What time is it? It's only 12:30," the man answered.

"The easiest time to add insult to injury is when you're signing someone's cast."
—DEMETRI MARTIN

Two men are discussing the ailing health of their parents.

"I feel bad," the first man says. "My dad is senile. All he does is stare through the window all day long."

"That's an awful way to live," the second man responds.

"Yeah, I know," the man admitted. "One day I should really let him in the house."

<hr/>

After a preacher died and went to heaven, he noticed a New York cab driver had been awarded a higher place than he. "I don't understand," he complained to God. "I devoted my entire life to my congregation."

God explained to him, "Our policy here in heaven is to reward results. Now, was your congregation well attuned to you whenever you gave a sermon?"

"Well," the minister had to admit, "some in the congregation fell asleep from time to time."

"Exactly," said God, "and when people rode in this man's taxi, they not only stayed awake, they even prayed."

Did you hear the good news about reincarnation? *It's making a comeback.*

A man dies and finds himself in front of God. He sees Jesus sitting at his right hand and a janitor with a mop sitting to his left. "Who are you?" the man asks the janitor.

"I'm Cleanliness."

"The inventor of the Etch A Sketch died last week. His family was shaken, but is now ready to start over."—CHRIS ILLUMINATI

A man places some flowers on the grave of his dearly departed mother and starts back toward his car when his attention is diverted to another man kneeling at a grave. The man seems to be praying with profound intensity and keeps repeating, "Why did you have to die? Why did you have to die?"

The first man approaches him and says, "Sir, I don't wish to interfere with your private grief, but this demonstration of pain is more than I've ever seen before. Who are you mourning? A child? A parent?"

The mourner takes a moment to collect himself, then replies, "My wife's first husband."

One dark night, two men are walking home after a party and decide to take a shortcut through the cemetery. Right in the middle of the cemetery they are startled by a tap-tap-tapping noise coming from the misty shadows. Trembling with fear, they find an old man with a hammer and chisel, chipping away at one of the headstones.

"Holy cow, dude," one says after catching his breath. "You scared us half to death. We thought you were a ghost! What are you doing, working here so late at night?"

"Those fools!" the old man grumbles. "They misspelled my name!"

"I am not afraid of death, I just don't want to be there when it happens."—WOODY ALLEN

A new business is opening and one of the owner's friends wants to send him flowers for the occasion. They arrive at the new business site and the owner reads the card: "Rest in Peace." Understandably the owner is angry and calls the florist to complain.

After he tells the florist of the obvious mistake and how angry he is, the florist replies, "Sir, I'm really sorry for the mistake, but rather than getting angry, you should imagine this. Somewhere there is a funeral taking place today, and they have flowers with a note saying, 'Congratulations on your new location.'"

———◆———

A husband calls for his wife on his deathbed. He tells his wife that after he passes away he doesn't want her to be alone. "Six months after I pass, I think it would be okay for you to marry Joe."

"Joe?" his wife asks. "But I thought you hated Joe."

"I do," the man answers.

———◆———

A cult of cannibals eats a car full of circus clowns. In the middle of the meal one cannibal turns to the other and asks, "Does this meal taste funny to you?"

———◆———

A father passes away and his son is arranging the funeral. He talks to the mortician about his father's remains.

The son says, "I know we don't have much money, but I want the best for my father. Please do what you can."

A week after the funeral, the mortician presents the son with a bill for fifty dollars. Thinking it to be very reasonable, the son pays the bill. The next week, the son gets another bill for fifty dollars from the mortician. He pays that as well. A week later a third bill arrives in the amount of fifty dollars.

The son calls the mortician and says. "The funeral was three weeks ago. Why am I still getting bills for fifty dollars?"

"You wanted the best for your father," the mortician says, "so that tux was rented."

"If you eat one apple a day for 80 years, you won't die young."—BLACKIE SHERROD

There once was an old man who worked in a whiskey distillery. One night, while working late, he tripped over his shoelaces and fell into a massive vat of booze. Six hours later he drowned. It really shouldn't have taken as long as it did for him to die, but he got out of the vat three times to take a leak.

A couple's happy married life almost goes completely wrong because of Aunt Emma. For seventeen long years, Aunt Emma has lived with them, always crotchety, always demanding. Finally, the old woman passes away. On the way back from the cemetery, the husband confesses to his wife, "Darling, if I didn't love you so much, I don't think I would have put up with having your Aunt Emma in the house all those years."

His wife looks at him in shock.

"My Aunt Emma?" she cries. "I thought she was your Aunt Emma!"

Two men are talking about how they want to leave the world.

"I'd like to go out like my uncle," says the first man. "He died at the racetrack."

The second man says he'd like to go out like his grandfather. "He just died peacefully. Fell asleep and never woke up or made a sound. Nothing like the people riding in his bus."

Chapter 8

FOUR-LEGGED FUNNIES:

Jokes about animals and pets

As every pet owner knows, our four-legged friends are part of the family. They eat with us (sometimes stealing food right off the dinner table), sleep with us, play with us, and use our front lawn as a bathroom. Yes, animals truly enrich our lives. Even those who don't like pets and animals very much will find something to chuckle over in the following jokes. After all, animals can be just as crazy and hilarious as their human counterparts. These amusing anecdotes and ridiculous gags are sure to make anyone smirk like the Cheshire Cat or laugh like a hyena.

A man angrily knocks on the door of a house. The homeowner answers and the man begins shouting, "Your dog jumped the fence, chased me on a bicycle, and bit my leg!"

The homeowner looks at the man and said, "That's impossible. My dog has no idea how to ride a bike."

"I bought myself a parrot, but it did not say 'I'm hungry,' and so it died."—
MITCH HEDBERG

There was a father mole, a mother mole, and a baby mole that lived in a hole out in the country not far from a farmhouse. One morning, the father mole poked his head out of the hole and said, "Mmmm, I think I smell sausage cooking!"

The mother mole pushed the father mole aside, poked her head outside the hole, and said, "Mmmm, I think I smell pancakes!"

The baby mole tried to push aside the two bigger moles to stick his head outside the hole, but couldn't, because he was so much smaller.

Frustrated, the baby mole said out loud, "The only thing I smell is molasses."

100% FARM RAISED

A pig walks into a bar, orders twenty beers, and starts chugging them all one by one. "That's impressive," says the bartender. "Want to know where the bathroom is?"

The pig replies, "No thanks, pal. I'm just going to go wee wee wee all the way home."

———◆———

How does an octopus go to war? *Very well armed.*

———◆———

Why was the duck arrested? *He was suspected of selling quack.*

———◆———

Did you hear about the breakdancing goldfish? *He could only do it for about twenty seconds.*

What did the father buffalo say to his kid before leaving for work every morning? *Bison.*

Two roaches are munching on garbage in an alley when one starts a discussion about a new restaurant.

"I was in that new restaurant across the street," says one. "It's so clean! The kitchen is spotless, and the floors are gleaming white. There is no dirt anywhere—it's so sanitary that the whole place shines."

"Please," says the other roach, frowning. "Not while I'm eating!"

Two flies land on a pile of manure. One fly passes gas. The other fly looks at him and says, "Hey do you mind? I'm eating here."

A man walks into a zoo. The only animal in the entire zoo is a dog. It's a shih tzu.

"To err is human; to purr, feline."
—ROBERT BYRNE

Two men, Jim and John, are walking their dogs when they pass by a restaurant.

"Let's go in and get something to eat," Jim suggests.

"We can't," responds John. "Don't you see the sign says *No Pets Allowed*?"

"Oh, that sign?" says Jim. "Don't worry about it."

Taking out a pair of sunglasses, he walks up to the door. As he tries walking into the restaurant, the host says, "Sorry, no pets allowed."

"Can't you see?" says Jim. "I am blind. This is my Seeing Eye dog."

"But it's a Doberman pinscher. Who uses a Doberman pinscher as a Seeing Eye dog?" the host asks.

"Oh," Jim responds, "you must not have heard. This is the latest type of Seeing Eye dog. They do a very good job."

Seeing that it worked, John tries walking in with his Chihuahua. Even before he can open his mouth, the host says, "Don't tell me that a Chihuahua is the latest type of Seeing Eye dog."

John responds angrily, "You mean they gave me a Chihuahua?"

"A bird in the hand makes blowing your nose difficult."—SOLOMON SHORT

A snake goes in to see the optometrist because his eyesight is failing.

"It's actually affecting my life. I can't hunt anymore because I can't see."

The doctor fits the snake for glasses and the snake immediately notices an improvement in his eyesight. A week later, the doctor calls the snake to check how the glasses are holding up.

"They're fine," the snake answers. "But now I'm being treated for depression."

"Depression?" the doctor asks.

"Yeah, my eyesight cleared up, but it made me realize I've been dating a garden hose."

———◆———

A mother bunny was shopping with her little bunny when finally she had enough of the little bunny's question. "A magician pulled you out of a hat! Now stop asking!"

Two ducks are having an affair. They rent a hotel room for an hour, but the male duck forgot contraception. He calls down to room service.

"Got it," says the front desk, "and would you like these on your bill?"

"Of course not," the duck says. "I'd suffocate."

"We've begun to long for the pitter-patter of little feet—so we bought a dog; well, it's cheaper, and you get more feet."—RITA RUDNER

Why don't blind people skydive? *It scares the crap out of the dog.*

Two cows are sitting in the field when one says, "Hey man, I've been hearing of bad stuff lately. Are you worried about this 'mad cow disease'?"

The other cow starts to spin around with his hooves extended out and says, "Not me, pal. I'm a helicopter."

A lady was expecting the plumber. He was scheduled to come at 10 A.M. Ten o'clock came and went with no plumber. She concluded he wasn't coming, and went out to do some errands. While she was out, the plumber arrived. He knocked on the door; the lady's parrot, who was at home in a cage by the door, said, "Who is it?"

He replied, "It's the plumber."

He thought it was the lady who'd said, "Who is it?" and waited for her to come and let him in.

When this didn't happen he knocked again, and again the parrot said, "Who is it?"

He said, "It's the plumber!" He waited, and again the lady didn't come to let him in.

He knocked again, and again the parrot said, "Who is it?"

He said, "It's the plumber!"

Again he waited and again she didn't come. He knocked again and the parrot said, "Who is it?"

The plumber screamed, flew into a rage, pushed the door in, and ripped it off its hinges. He suffered a heart attack and fell dead in the doorway. The lady came home from her errands, only to see the door ripped off its hinges and a corpse lying in the doorway. "A dead body!" she exclaimed. "Who is it?"

The parrot said, "It's the plumber."

"I ask people why they have deer heads on their walls. They always say because it's such a beautiful animal. There you go. I think my mother is attractive, but I have photographs of her."—ELLEN DEGENERES

A chicken walks over to a duck standing on the side of the road. The duck is considering crossing to the other side.

"Don't do it, pal," the chicken says. "You'll never hear the end of it."

Three vampire bats live in a cave surrounded by three castles. One night, the bats bet on who can drink the most blood. The first bat comes home with blood dripping off his fangs.

He says, "See that castle over there? I drank the blood of three people."

The second bat returns with blood around his mouth. He says, "See that castle over there? I drank the blood of five people."

The third bat comes back covered in blood. He says, "See that castle over there?" The other bats nod. "Well," says the third bat, "I didn't."

> ## "My wife kisses the dog on the lips yet won't even drink from my glass."
> —RODNEY DANGERFIELD

What do you get when you cross a lion with a parrot? *No idea, but when that animal talks, people will listen.*

Dave went to the store for a box of mothballs. His closet was infested with moths and he needed a solution. The next day, Dave returned to buy five more boxes.

"Weren't you just here yesterday to buy a box of mothballs?" the store clerk asked.

"Yes, but I used up that box already. Those suckers are hard to hit when they start moving!"

Why did the chicken say, "Meow, oink, bow-wow, moo"? *He was studying foreign languages.*

Two farmers are standing in a field discussing their work.

"I'm having an issue with my flock of cows," the first farmer admits.

"Herd of cows," the second farmer corrects his friend.

"Of course I've heard of cows," the first farmer barks, "I've got a whole flock of them!"

———◆·◆———

What did the grape say when an elephant stepped on it?
Nothing, it just let out a little whine.

———◆·◆———

"Julie," her mother asked, "why are you feeding birdseed to the cat?"

"Because," Julie answered, "that's where my canary is."

———◆·◆———

A man rings the doorbell of a small house and an old woman answers.

"I'm sorry," the man says, "but I'm afraid I've run over your cat. I'd like to replace it if I can."

"All right," the old woman says. "But how good are you at catching mice?"

A couple's house is infested with flies. While waiting for the exterminator, the husband goes around the house on a mission to kill as many flies as possible.

"Well," he says to his wife, "I killed six flies. Four were male and two were female."

"How can you tell the sex?" she asks.

"Four of the flies were on a beer can and the other two were on the phone."

"The most affectionate creature in the world is a wet dog."—AMBROSE BIERCE

A boy asks his father for a spider for his birthday. The father stops by the pet shop on the way home from work to find out more about spiders.

"What does one of those big ones cost?" the father asks, pointing into the glass case full of the arachnids.

"About fifty dollars," the store clerk replies.

"Fifty dollars!" the father replies. "I'll just find a cheap one off the web."

———◆———

What do bees say about the summer weather? *Swarm.*

———◆———

Why did the eagle grow his claws so long? *He wanted to enter a local talon contest.*

———◆———

Al bragged about his home aquarium to a friend.

"I keep it super clean," he said. "And my fish are always so darn happy."

"How the heck can you tell your fish are happy?" his friend asked.

"Because," Al replied, "they are always wagging their tails."

———◆———

A grasshopper walks into a crowded bar. He sits down on a stool and orders a glass of beer. The bartender says, "That's funny. I figured you'd order something different, especially since we've got a drink named after you."

The grasshopper looks at the bartender baffled and says, "You've got a drink named Stan?"

A man is sitting on his couch watching TV when he hears the doorbell ring. He opens the door, and all he can see is a snail sitting on his front porch. He throws the snail across the street and goes back to watching TV. A year later, he is again sitting on his couch watching TV when the doorbell rings. He opens the door to see an angry snail, who yells, "What the heck was that for?"

What is the number one cause of death for hamsters?
Falling asleep at the wheel.

Two bats are hanging upside down in a cave. The first bat asks the second, "Do you remember the worst day of your life?"

The second bat replies "I sure do. It was the day I had diarrhea."

A kangaroo keeps escaping his enclosure at the zoo. In an effort to keep him inside at night, the zookeepers construct a 10-foot fence around his habitat. The next morning, they find the kangaroo wandering around the zoo. The zookeepers construct a 20-foot fence to keep the kangaroo from escaping, but the next day he is loose once again. The zookeepers begin construction on a 50-foot fence they're sure will keep the kangaroo in his enclosure. Watching the men work, a camel in the neighboring enclosure sticks his head over to the kangaroo's side and asks, "How high do you think they'll make it this time?"

The kangaroo answers, "Not sure, but it still won't matter, unless they remember to lock the door this time."

———⬦———

A zookeeper stumbles across a man throwing five-dollar bills into the monkey cage.

"What the heck are you doing?" the zookeeper asks.

"The signs says it's cool," the man answers, pointing to a sign in front of the cages.

"No, it doesn't," the zookeeper replies.

"Sure it does," says the man, tossing another bill in the cage. "It says, 'Do Not Feed Monkeys. $5 Fine.'"

"If it's so great outside, why are all the bugs trying to get in my house?"—JIM GAFFIGAN

Did you hear about the leopard constantly trying to escape the national zoo? *It never works; he's always spotted.*

A blind man is walking down the street with his Seeing Eye dog. They stop at the corner to wait for the traffic light to change. The dog, unable to wait any longer, begins peeing on the blind man's leg. After the dog finishes, the blind man reaches into his coat pocket and pulls out a doggie treat. He holds it out for the dog. A pedestrian standing next to the blind man sees the entire event and he's shocked. He turns to the blind man and says, "Why would you reward your dog for peeing on your leg?"

The blind man replies, "Oh I'm not rewarding him, I'm just trying to find his head so I can kick him in the butt."

How did the fish get high? *He's got a connection for really good seaweed.*

A woman calls the vet because her beloved dog isn't moving. The vet makes a house call and after a quick examination tells the woman her dog is going to die.

"Isn't there anything you can do?" the woman pleads with the vet. He thinks it over, leaves the room, and returns with her cat. The cat sniffs the dog head to toe, looks him over, and shakes his head at the vet.

"I'm sorry, miss. It's out of our hands." The vet hands the woman a bill for $1,570 before he leaves.

"What?" the woman screams. "How is the bill $1,570? You didn't do anything."

"Well," replies the vet, "it's $70 for the consultation, $100 for the house call, and $1,400 for the emergency cat scan."

A farmer spends $7,000 on a young registered Black Angus bull to mate with his cows. He puts the bull out with the herd, but the animal just eats grass. He won't even look at the cows. The farmer feels cheated, so he brings in the local vet to check out the bull. The bull is very healthy, the vet explains, but possibly just a little young. So he gives the farmer pills to feed the bull once per day. It will help with his urge to mate. After a few days, the bull starts to service a few cows, and within a week, every cow on the farm. The bull even breaks through the fence and breeds with all of the neighbor's cows. He turns into a mating machine. A friend of the farmer asks exactly what the vet gave the bull to cause such a drastic change.

"I don't know exactly what was in those pills," the farmer says. "All I can tell you is they work and they taste like peppermint."

A man is telling a bartender about the craziest day of his life.

"It was unreal," the man recalls. "I'm on this horse that's galloping at top speed. On the right side of me is this elephant going as fast as the horse. Right in front of us is another horse going just fast enough so we don't hit him, and about ten feet behind us is a lion giving chase. He could catch us at any minute!"

The bartender is in shock. "My God," he says to man. "What did you do?"

"Well, I had no choice," the man replies, taking a sip of his beer. "I got my drunk butt off that merry-go-round as fast as possible."

"'You scratch my back, and I'll suck blood out of yours.' That is the insect motto."—DAVE BARRY

A man on vacation in the Caribbean decides to go horseback riding. He visits a local farm that rents horses to ride around the countryside. The owner of the horse, a very religious man, explains to the visitor that in order to make the horse go, he'll have to say "Thank God," and to make the horse stop, he should say "Amen." During his ride around the village, the horse is stung by a bee. In pain and shock, the horse takes off running right toward a dangerous cliff.

"Amen!" the man shouts, hanging on to the horse for dear life. The horse stops just a few inches short of the cliff's edge. The man catches his breath, looks over the cliff, and mutters out loud, "Thank God."

What's the difference between deer nuts and beer nuts?
Beer nuts are a dollar seventy-five and deer nuts are always under a buck.

———◆———

A dog walks into an employment agency and says he's looking for full-time work. "Holy cow! A talking dog!" the agency owner cries. "With your talent, I'm sure we could find you a job in entertainment. Maybe a circus?"

"A circus?" the dog asks. "Why would the circus need an accountant?"

———◆———

After returning from a trip from the Sunshine State, a man tells his friend all the things he'd seen. "Did you know in Florida they use alligators to make handbags?"

His friend says in amazement, "Wow, it's crazy what they can make animals do these days."

———◆———

A burglar breaks into a house late at night. He's going through all of the family's belongings when he hears a voice say, "Jesus is watching you."

He looks around and sees no one, and thinks he's imagining things. He goes back to what he's doing and again hears a voice say, "Jesus is watching you."

He shines his flashlight on a parrot in a cage across the room. "Are you the one saying 'Jesus is watching me'?" he asks the parrot.

"Yes," the parrot replies.

"What's your name?" the burglar asks.

"My name is Clarence."

"Clarence?" the burglar laughs. "That's a dumb name for a parrot. What idiot named you Clarence?"

The parrot answers, "The same idiot who named his pit bull Jesus."

"You know when they have a fishing show on TV, they catch the fish and then let it go. They don't want to eat the fish, they just want to make it late for something."—MITCH HEDBERG

A man buys a talking parrot from the local pet shop. He takes the parrot home and tries to teach the parrot to say a few things. Instead of repeating him, the parrot just swears at the man. After a few aggravating hours of the same responses from the parrot, the man threatens the bird with a severe punishment.

"If you don't stop swearing, I'm going to put you in the freezer."

The parrot continues to curse, so the man has no choice but to put him in the freezer. About a half hour later, the man opens the door to find the parrot happy to see him but freezing cold.

"Have you learned your lesson?" the man asks.

"I sure have," the parrot replies. "I promise never to swear again."

After thawing out for a moment, the parrot turns to the man and asks, "So what did the turkey in there do to you?"

A lost dog strays into a jungle. A lion sees this from a distance and says with caution, "This guy looks edible; never seen his kind before." So the lion starts rushing toward the dog with menace. The dog notices and starts to panic, but as he's about to run he sees some bones next to him and gets an idea. He says loudly, "Mmm . . . that was some good lion meat!"

The lion abruptly stops and says, "Whoa! This guy seems tougher than he looks. I'd better leave while I can."

From a nearby treetop, a monkey witnesses everything. The monkey realizes that he can benefit from this situation by telling the lion and getting something in return, so he proceeds to tell the lion what really happened. The lion says angrily, "Get on my back, we'll get him together." They start rushing back to the dog. The dog sees them and, realizing what has happened, starts to panic even more.

He then gets another idea and shouts, "Where the hell is that monkey! I told him to bring me another lion an hour ago!"

Chapter 9

DAILY LAUGH:

Jokes about everyday absurdities

L egendary comedian Will Rogers once said, "Everything is funny as long as it is happening to somebody else." Daily life is full of hilarious little moments everyone can relate to. We've all been the boob who's locked his keys in his car at least once. Laughing about everyday frustrations makes life a little easier and helps us connect to each other. Even through life's sticky, unfortunate occurrences, it's all okay in the end as long as we can laugh together! Here are some jokes about everyday life that will have you and your friends in stitches.

A man is stuck inside a public restroom without any toilet paper. He calls over to the man in the next stall, "Hey, you got any extra toilet paper in there?"

"No," replies the man.

"You got any newspaper over there?" the stranded man asks.

"Nope," the second man replies.

After a moment of silence, the first man asks the second, "You got two fives for a ten?"

———————

Two priests are standing by the side of the road holding up a sign that reads, "The End is Near! Turn yourself around now before it's too late!" They plan to hold up the sign to each passing car.

"Leave us alone, you religious nuts!" yells the first driver as he speeds by. From around the curve the priests hear screeching tires and a big splash.

"Do you think," one priest says to other, "it would be better to shorten the sign to 'Bridge Out' instead?"

"A word to the wise isn't necessary. It's the stupid ones that need the advice."—BILL COSBY

Two men are walking side by side down the street. One of them sees a broken piece of mirror on the ground, grabs it, looks at it, and says, "This guy looks so familiar, but I can't remember where I know him from."

The other guy grabs it from his hand, takes a look at it, and says, "It's me, you idiot!"

The past, present, and future walk into a bar. It was tense.

How many American tourists does it take to change a light bulb? *Fifteen. Five to figure out how much the bulb costs in the local currency, four to comment on "how funny-looking" local light bulbs are, three to hire a local person to change the bulb, two to take pictures, and one to buy postcards in case the pictures don't come out.*

"I hope we find a cure for every major disease because I'm tired of walking in 5Ks."

—DANIEL TOSH

A man finishes pumping gas and goes into the store to pay. A sign on the pumps says, "Please tell cashier the pump number to pay." The man walks up to the counter and says to the clerk, "Number 2." The clerk hands the man a set of keys, motions to a hallway next to the counter, and says, "The second door on the left."

———◆———

You might be a redneck if your daughter's sweet sixteen is sponsored by Budweiser.

———◆———

If you think nobody cares you are alive, try missing a couple of payments.

———◆———

A clear conscience is usually the sign of a bad memory.

———◆———

Two rednecks are walking along when they see a dog licking his genitals. The first redneck says, "I wish I could do that."

The other responds, "If you tried, he'd probably bite you."

———————

What do you call someone who speaks three languages? Multilingual.

What do you call someone who speaks two languages? Bilingual.

What do you call someone who speaks one language? An American.

———————

What did the two iPhones say to the two iPads? *"Want to get kinky and have a 4G?"*

———————

Why are tall people always so well rested? *They sleep longer in bed.*

———————

What did the head of the nudist colony say to the newest male members? *"The first is always the hardest."*

Did you hear the rumor about exit signs? *They are on the way out.*

"One of my college friends has a stutter and a lot of people think it's a bad thing, but to me it's just like starting certain words with a drum roll. That's not an impediment, that's suspense."—DEMETRI MARTIN

How did the hipster burn his tongue? *He tried to eat his food before it was cool.*

Did you know 50 percent of people use Google as a search engine and the other 50 percent use it to check to see if their Internet is connected?

Change your Facebook name to Benefits so when someone adds you on Facebook, it will say, "You are now friends with Benefits."

A man was eating in a restaurant when he desperately needed to pass gas. The music was really, really loud, so he timed his gas with the beat of the music. After a couple of songs, he started to feel better. He finished his coffee and noticed that everybody was staring at him. Then he suddenly remembered he was listening to his iPod.

"There's no better feeling in the world than a warm pizza box on your lap."—KEVIN JAMES

A policeman came to my door yesterday and asked, "Where were you between four and six?"

So I said, "Probably either in kindergarten or first grade."

How do you make antifreeze? *Steal her blankets.*

A woman is getting lunch ready when the phone rings. "This is the middle school calling about your son Phillip. He's been caught telling unbelievable lies."

"I'll say he has," the woman replies. "I don't have a son."

A man bought a self-help book from the bookstore. The title of the book was *How to Handle Life's Biggest Disappointments*. When he opened the book to read it that night he realized all the pages were blank.

"A day without sunshine is like, you know, night."—STEVE MARTIN

A bride is going over the wedding planning with her mother. "I've got something new and something borrowed, but I don't have anything old or blue."

"Don't worry," the mother says, "your father's mother is coming and she hasn't paid her heating bill in months."

———◆———

Did you hear about the man who received a life sentence just for one day of bobsleighing? *He killed twenty Bobs in one day.*

———◆———

Did you hear about the new garlic and onions diet? *You eat nothing but garlic and onions for a week. You don't lose much weight, but people will be standing so far away you'll appear smaller.*

———◆———

"I saw a recent picture of you," a brother tells his sister who lives halfway around the world, "and I've got to be honest—you're looking kind of big."

"That's an awful thing to say!" the sister barks. "And where did you see a photo of me?"

"Google Earth," the brother answers.

———◆———

The CEO of a major corporation is asked to give an address to shareholders at the yearly meeting. He asks the company press officer to write him a twenty-minute speech. When the CEO returns from the convention, he is furious at the press officer.

"Are you trying to kill my career?" the CEO barks. "I asked for a twenty-minute speech and you give me an hour-long speech. People were standing up and walking out."

"No," says the press officer, "I gave you exactly what you requested—a twenty-minute speech and two extra copies."

What's the worst part about sitting in traffic? *Getting run over.*

What goes *click*, "How about now?" *click*, "How about now?" *click*, "How about now?" *A blind man attempting to solve a Rubik's Cube.*

A hangover is the wrath of grapes.

Fart in church and you'll end up sitting in your own pew.

A woman was driving in rush-hour traffic when the car in front of her stopped suddenly. She didn't have time to brake and smashed right into the car's back bumper. A dwarf got out of the driver's seat and approached the woman's car angrily. "I'm not happy!" the dwarf said through her closed window.

The woman rolled down the window and replied, "Good. My neck hurts, so I was hoping you were Doc."

"When life hands you lemons, make whiskey sours."—W.C. FIELDS

While watching a movie in the theater, a man can't hear the dialogue over the chatter of the two women sitting in front of him. Unable to bear it any longer, he taps one of them on the shoulder. "Excuse me," he says, "I can't hear."

"I should hope not," one woman replies sharply. "This is a private conversation."

A drunk man hails a taxi cab. When the taxi pulls over, the drunk sticks his head in the passenger side window and asks the driver, "Have you got room in here for a whole lobster and three bottles of wine?"

"Sure," replies the driver.

The drunk man says, "Fantastic!" and throws up on the passenger seat.

A drunk man stared at a huge billboard for more than an hour. The billboard, advertising soda, wanted the world to Drink Canada Dry. So the drunk bought a bus ticket to give it a shot.

A lady walks into a dress shop one afternoon after spotting a gorgeous strapless dress in the shop window. She tells the store clerk, "I'd like to try on that strapless dress in the window."

The store clerk replies, "You can try on the dress, miss, but I think the changing room would be a much better place to do it."

"Life is one long process of getting tired."
—SAMUEL BUTLER

Three convicts escape from jail and are being chased by police. They turn onto a dark alley and spot a bunch of potato sacks. Each of the three hides in one. A policeman quickly comes through the scene and hears a rustling from the potato sacks. He goes over to them and kicks the first potato sack.

"Meow!" says a convict. The policeman goes to the next one muttering, "Stupid cats."

He kicks the second potato sack and the second convict says, "Woof!"

"Stupid dogs!" says the policeman while moving on to the next potato sack. The policeman kicks it. Nothing happens. So he kicks it again and the last convict says, "Potato, potato!"

A lady on a commuter train is reading a newspaper article about life and death statistics.

Fascinated, she turns to the man next to her and asks, "Did you know that every time I breathe somebody dies?"

"Really?" he said. "Have you tried a good mouthwash?"

"There are three things in life that people like to stare at: a flowing stream, a crackling fire, and a Zamboni clearing the ice."—CHARLIE BROWN

Three men are convicted of a crime and sentenced to twenty years in solitary confinement. They're each allowed to bring something into the cell. The first man chooses as many books as can fit in the cell. The second man requests painting supplies. The last man requests twenty years' worth of cigarettes. On the morning of their release, the warden goes to visit each man in his cell.

The first man tells the warden, "These last twenty years of studying have been amazing. I'm going to go back to school and get my teaching degree."

The second man tells the warden, "I've become an accomplished artist and my works will hang in some of the most famous galleries in the world."

The warden enters the third man's cell and finds him surrounded by all of the cigarettes. The man tells the warden, "I probably should have also requested matches."

A man is driving home, drunk as a skunk. Suddenly he has to swerve to avoid a tree, then another, then another. A police car pulls him over as he veers all over the road. The drunk tells the cop about all the trees in the road.

The cop says, "For God's sake! That's your pine tree air freshener swinging about."

"I owe it all to little chocolate donuts."
—JOHN BELUSHI

Just before boarding began, a flight attendant announced that the flight was overbooked. She explained that the airline was looking for volunteers to give up their seats. In exchange, the airline would offer a $100 voucher for the next flight and a First Class ticket for the plane leaving a few hours later. A small group of people ran up to the counter to take advantage of the offer. A few minutes later, all of the people returned to their seats with angry looks on their faces. The flight attendant got back on the intercom and announced, "If there is anyone besides the flight crew who'd like to volunteer, come up to the desk."

The town drunk stumbles over to a parking meter, stands in front of it, and reads that there are sixty minutes left until it expires.

"I don't believe it!" he cries out. "I've lost 100 pounds!"

A prisoner finishes a thirty-year sentence and is released from jail. The moment he's outside the prison walls, he begins to jump up and down and scream out, "I'm free! I'm free!"

A little boy riding his bike past the prison grounds yells out to the ex-con, "Big deal! I'm four!"

"Some mornings, it's just not worth chewing through the leather straps."—EMO PHILIPS

A man releases a genie from a bottle and is granted only two wishes.

"Fine," says the man, "I can live with just two wishes. I'll take the best wine in the world and best woman in the world as my wife."

In a flash, the man had a bottle of the best wine money could buy. Unfortunately, he'd have to share it with his new wife, Mother Teresa.

Fifteen minutes into a cross-country flight, the plane's captain announces over the intercom, "Ladies and gentlemen, one of our engines has failed. There is nothing to worry about. Our flight will take an hour longer than scheduled, but we still have three engines left."

Thirty minutes later the captain announces, "Ladies and gentlemen, one more engine has failed and the flight will take an additional two hours. But don't worry. We can fly just fine on two engines."

An hour later the captain announces, "Ladies and gentlemen, one more engine has failed and our arrival will be delayed another three hours. But don't worry. We still have one engine left."

A young passenger turns to the man in the next seat and remarks, "If we lose one more engine, we'll be up here all day."

A drunk man arrives for his day in court. He appears before the judge, who looks down at his case file and says, "You've been brought here for drinking."

The drunk man smiles widely and says, "Great! Let's start the drinking!"

"Some of the worst mistakes of my life have been haircuts."—JIM MORRISON

After a two-week criminal trial in a very high-profile bank robbery case, the jury finally ends its fourteen hours of deliberations and enters the courtroom to deliver its verdict to the judge. The judge turns to the jury foreman and asks, "Has the jury reached a verdict in this case?"

"Yes we have, your honor," the foreman responds.

"Would you please pass it to me," the judge declares, and motions for the bailiff to retrieve the verdict slip from the foreman and deliver it to him. After the judge reads the verdict himself, he delivers the verdict slip back to his bailiff to be returned to the foreman and instructs the foreman, "Please read your verdict to the court."

"We find the defendant not guilty of all four counts of bank robbery," states the foreman.

The family and friends of the defendant jump for joy at the sound of the "not guilty" verdict and hug each other as they shout expressions of gratitude. The defendant's attorney turns to his client and asks, "So, what do you think about that?"

The defendant looks around the courtroom slowly with a bewildered look on his face and then turns to his defense attorney and says, "I'm real confused here. Does this mean that I have to give all the money back?"

A guy walks into a bar and grabs a stool. Before he can order a drink, the bowl of pretzels on the bar in front of him says, "Hey, you're a handsome fellow."

The man tries to ignore the bowl of pretzels and orders a drink from the bartender. The bowl of pretzels tries to get the man's attention again by saying, "Ooh, a pilsner, that's a great choice. You seem like an incredibly smart man."

Getting very uncomfortable with the pretzel's comments, the guy says to the bartender, "Hey, what the heck is up with this bowl of pretzels? It just keeps saying really nice things about me."

The bartender says, "It's normal. The pretzels are complimentary."

"When I was young I used to think that money was the most important thing in life; now that I am old, I know it is."
—OSCAR WILDE

Two classmates are discussing the current state of their alma mater at a reunion weekend barbecue. "Things have really gotten crazy here," the first man says. "Did you know the football coach makes three times the salary as the head of the English department?"

The second man responds, "Well, that kind of makes sense. I'm pretty sure 100,000 screaming fans wouldn't show up on Saturday for a lecture on Shakespeare."

Did you hear about the social studies teacher fired for being cross-eyed? *He couldn't control his pupils.*

Looking out into the pitch-black night, a sea captain sees a light dead ahead. It's on a collision course with his ship.

He sends out a light signal: "Change your course ten degrees east."

The light signals back to the ship, "Change yours ten degrees west."

Angrily, the captain sends a second signal, stating, "I'm a navy captain! Change your course, sir!"

"I'm a seaman, second class," comes back in reply. "You change your course, sir."

The captain is now furious. "I'm a battleship!" he signals. "I'm not changing course for anything."

He receives one final call, stating, "Well, I'm a lighthouse, so it's your call."

"The poor wish to be rich, the rich wish to be happy, the single wish to be married, and the married wish to be dead."—ANN LANDERS

A man walks into a bar and tells the bartender he'd like something tall, icy, and full of vodka. The bartender holds up his finger for the man to wait a minute and yells into the back room, "Hey Tiffany, someone is here looking for you!"

———◆———

A woman calls her husband's cell phone to tell him the car is giving her a problem. She thinks there is water in the carburetor.

"How the heck would you know that?" the husband asks.

"Because I just drove it into a canal."

A pastor was enraged when he found a bill for a $250 dress in his wife's purse. "How could you do this?" the pastor cried. "You know we're on an incredibly tight budget!"

"I know," the woman said, "but the devil himself was shopping with me. He convinced me the dress looked so good I had to buy it!"

The pastor consoled his wife with a hand on her shoulder. "In those moments, my love, you've got to yell out loud, 'Get behind me, Satan!'"

"I did that," the wife explained, "and he said, 'The dress even looks good from back here.'"

"Live each day as if it were your last . . . because one day, you'll be right."—BENNY HILL

A drunk man falls down the front steps of the W Hotel in New York. He lands at the feet of a cab driver waiting for his next fare. The drunk man stands up and says, "Take me to the W Hotel!"

The cabby looks at the drunk man and tells him, "Buddy, you're at the W Hotel."

Perfect," the man says, handing the driver a twenty-dollar bill, "but next time don't drive so fast."

One evening an old farmer decides to go down to his pond. He hasn't been there in months, and feels the urge to check on things. As he gets closer, he hears loud giggling coming from the pond. He is shocked to find a bunch of young women skinny-dipping.

"Hey, what's going on here?" he shouts, alerting the women who were standing at the water's edge. All of the women scream in shock and swim to the deep end of the pond. One of the women shouts to the farmer, "We're not coming out until you leave, you pervert!"

The old man replies, "I didn't come down here to watch you ladies swim or see you naked! I'm here to feed the alligator!"

———◆———

A diet guru is holding a seminar in the conference room of a large hotel. "The food we eat," he explains, "is slowly killing us. Red meats attack the heart. Vegetables and fruits are sprayed with harmful pesticides. Even our drinking water is polluted! But do you know which food is much more dangerous than them all? Can anyone tell me what it is?"

A man in the back of the room raises his hand and, when called on, answers, "Wedding cake?"

"Drama is life with the dull bits left out."
—ALFRED HITCHCOCK

A man is driving to work when he notices the flash of a traffic camera. He figures that his picture had been taken for exceeding the limit, even though he knows that he wasn't speeding. Just to be sure, he circles the block and passes the exact same spot, driving even slower this time through. Again, the camera flashes. He thinks it is hilarious, since he was obviously doing nothing wrong, so he drives even slower as he passes through the light for a third time. The traffic camera takes his photo again. He does it a fourth and fifth time and is hysterical each time when the camera flash snaps his picture. The final time he passes through the light he is going 20 miles under the speed limit. Two weeks later, he gets five tickets in the mail for operating a car without a safety belt.

A man was complaining about the local police to his neighbor.

"I'm sick of the cops in this town telling me how to drive when they are some of the worst drivers in the state."

"How do you know that?" the neighbor asks.

"Every week, I constantly pass signs on the side of the road that say *Police, Accident.*"

A young woman goes to a fortuneteller. The fortuneteller tells her that she will be broke and unhappy until she turns fifty.

"What happens when I turn fifty?" the young woman asks, staring down at the cards.

"Oh, nothing," said the fortuneteller. "You'll just be used to it by then."

———◆———

There are only two kinds of people in the world. There are those who wake up in the morning and say, "Good morning, Lord," and there are those who wake up in the morning and say, "Good Lord, it's morning."

"If only we'd stop trying to be happy we could have a pretty good time."—EDITH WHARTON

A man spends the entire night getting hammered at his local pub. After last call, the man stands up from his stool but falls flat on his face trying to walk. He pulls himself up in the doorway of the bar, attempts to stand, but falls flat on his face to the sidewalk. He drags himself to his car and drives home. He tries to unlock his front door, finally gets it unlocked, but falls flat on his face in the hallway of his home. His wife is standing on the steps to the bedroom, waiting for the man. "You've been out drinking again, haven't you?"

"What makes you say that?" the man asks, still lying on the cold wooden floor.

"Because the bar called. You forgot your wheelchair again!"